CALLING THE ELDERS

Reclaiming and Transforming Our Communities through Elder Wisdom

A Guide and Toolkit for Developing Local Councils of Elders

Maaskelah K. Thomas, PhD

Calling the Elders - Reclaiming and Transforming Our Communities through Elder Wisdom: A Guide and Toolkit for Developing Local Councils of Elders
Copyright © 2010 by Maaskelah K. Thomas PhD
Published by Transformative Concepts
Wichita, Kansas 67214
www.transformativeconcepts.com

Printed in the United States of America

Dedication

This Guide is dedicated, first and foremost, to Divine Spirit and to all the ancestors who have joined together with that Spirit and continue to love, lead and guide us during our sojourn on this plane. Chief among those, for me, are my beloved mother Wilda Berthina and my father, Baba Jihad Talib Rounds-Muqtasid – the first Presiding Elder of The African American Council of Elders ~ Wichita/Sedgwick County.
In addition, this Guide is dedicated to the founding, current and future members of The African American Council of Elders ~ Wichita/Sedgwick County, of which I someday hope to be a full member.

Finally, I dedicate this guide to the diasporic African community --- wherever its members may be found --- that we might continue to work to build and rebuild empowering institutions based on Kujichagulia/Self-determination for all our current and future generations.
To our blessed continuance…..

Power of Love

Adinkra Symbols

West African adinkra symbols represent popular proverbs and maxims, record historical events, express particular attitudes or behavior related to depicted figures, or concepts uniquely related to abstract shapes. Those shown in the plate below represent only a few. The symbol included on the cover of this guide is one of several symbols representing "Sankofa." It is often associated with the proverb, *"Se wo were fi na wosankofa a yenkyi,"* which translates *"It is not wrong to go back for that which you have forgotten."*

Table of Contents

(Tools and Resources to Start You on Your Journey!)

Collective Sankofa: Going back to get it together!

Introduction

"The Mbongi (Council) takes all problems of the community."[1]

Calling the elders!
Antonio is a freshman in high school. He's just been arrested and released after being involved in a fight with another youth at his school. A condition of his release, under a diversion protocol, is that he commit to regular school attendance, and improve his academic scores (he is an above-average math and science student, but is barely making it through English and History). He has to complete a conflict resolution course offered at the neighborhood center, and must not get any bad disciplinary reports from either his parents or his school. If he can fulfill these conditions, his record will be wiped clean of the arrest. However, if he cannot, he runs the risk of being placed out-of-home in a more structured disciplinary environment. Antonio's mother is a single parent, working a job and a half to support Antonio and his two younger sisters. She is a high school graduate, with a year of college, but never completed her post-high school education after becoming pregnant with Antonio, whose father left soon after he was born. His two younger sisters have a different father, who is not active in their lives either. She doesn't really have the time or resources to strictly monitor Antonio, who is not a "bad" kid, but doesn't really have the kind of structure at home that allows him to fully develop. Antonio's mother wants him to succeed at his diversion, but worries that she won't be able to provide the structure and support he needs, based on her work hours.

Enter the elders: Through a cooperative agreement with the county's Juvenile Justice Authority, the Council has agreed to assist Antonio and his family to meet the requirements of his diversion in a number of ways. But most important, they exemplify the values like truth, honesty, balance, justice, reciprocity, and self-knowledge. They help him regain his mind and envision a reality beyond his current circumstances. They make it a family thing, and extend the support of the community to the entire family, with full intention of bringing them through and keeping them strong, in order to entrust them with our continuance.

---

[1] Fu-Kiau, K. K. B (2007) Mbongi: An African traditional political institution. Atlanta: Afrikan Djeli Publishers.

The Council commission that focuses on youth issues meets with Antonio and his family to get a sense of their circumstances. Next, they work with Antonio to find out if he has goals beyond the diversion, and what those are. The commission then goes deeper to find and collect information regarding the school system, Antonio's neighborhood and other factors that may be impacting his behavior. After presenting their report to the larger Council, which debates and deliberates, the Council and Antonio's family develop accountability agreements --- Council members connect the family with community resources that can assist in Antonio's success: a mentor, a tutor for English and History, transportation to and from the community center, and even childcare and enrichment activities for his younger sisters while he is occupied with studies and counseling. In addition, the Council connects Antonio's mother with a parenting support group and parent mentor, to provide some support for her efforts at raising her three children. And through the elders personal and professional connections they are able to assist her to find more lucrative employment, so that toward the end of the six-month diversion period, she is able to give up her part-time job. Further, the Council reviews pertinent school district policies and practices to determine if there are areas for advocacy to assist Antonio and other students from the community. For the most part, the Council does not provide any of these services directly, but through relationships that they've built with resource providers in the community, they are able to make appropriate referrals and follow-up on those referrals regularly. When problems arise, they work with Antonio's family and the resource providers to resolve them. Everyone is focused on achieving success for Antonio and his family, and by extension, the community.

Calling the elders!

In the community where the Council serves, there are at least two dozen human service agencies and organizations providing services that range from youth development to ex-offender release programs. All of the organizations have as part of their mission to provide culturally appropriate programming for residents of this predominantly black community. All struggle regularly with financial resources to deliver their services, but rarely is anyone turned away who needs help. Some of the agencies and organizations offer the same or similar services, with their own special focus, for example, there are three substance abuse treatment agencies, but one focuses primarily on women's recovery, another focuses on ex-offender drug treatment and the other has had great success working with teens. In addition, one of the youth development organizations is skilled at employing computer technology and Internet social networking to enhance services, and another has an outstanding grant writer. A funding opportunity is on the horizon for a comprehensive community development initiative; however, no single organization in the community can truthfully say they have the organizational capacity to fulfill the requirements of the grant. On the other hand, there is a large white agency in the city that could probably fulfill the requirements, but they have not previously expressed a commitment to culturally appropriate programming, and in fact, only have one black employee in the agency. The Council calls a meeting of all of the organizations, and together, they go through a facilitated process to identify strengths, challenges and resources available within the community. Together, they develop guiding principles for how they can work together and with potential service recipients, develop strategies for cross-referrals and supportive services for each agency. Through a process of open dialogue and honest communication, they are able to ultimately develop cooperative agreements for working together. Based on this, a lead organization is chosen to apply for the funding, with several of the other organizations included as collaborative partners. They agree that, whether or not they are awarded the grant, they will stay committed to working collaboratively to meet the needs of those they serve. A special commission of the Council is assigned and commits to the task of bring the group together regularly to review needs, issues, and opportunities for training, funding and other capacity-building efforts.

Calling the elders!

A proposed City-sponsored community development project will create new housing and commercial development in an older area of the community in much need of rehabilitation. An out-of-state urban planning consultant has proposed a plan that would displace and out-price many of the current residents in the area. A local planning consultant familiar with the community has proposed a plan that will build on the natural rhythm of the neighborhoods, concerned with maintain a balance between the new and the traditional, focusing on families and extended families. Neighborhood residents request an opportunity to review and comment on both proposals, but the City is reticent to open up the process and have tentatively chosen the out-of-state contractor based on their extensive work on similar projects. After taking their concerns to the Council, the elders lead and support community residents to demand that the City meet with them in the neighborhood, and present both plans for public comment. The City concedes, and after hearing passionate but rational concerns presented by the neighborhood residents, the City agrees to set up and train a local development group made up of at least half neighborhood residents to negotiate with the out-of-state consultant to mentor the local consultant and others, with the understanding that the project will stay under local, community control and residents will have a voice in the development project.

Is this your community? Could it be? As we move further into a new millennium, it is critical that we not leave behind those things and resources that have been so instrumental in the survival of black families over time. The elders are one of those resources. Are we utilizing the elders in our communities to assist efforts at community and family strengthening? Or, are we missing the opportunity to take advantage of what has historically been one of our most valuable resources?

Yeo, et al (1999)[2] performed a cohort analysis of African American elders through the ages, going back to 1900, to provide a sense of the historical markers that have impacted the lives of African Americans, and thus, what history elders from a range of age group cohorts hold as knowledge based on lived experiences. This rich reservoir of knowledge is an asset that can be drawn upon to frame the contemporary experiences of black people in our local communities and throughout our nation. Today's elders, age 55 and older, have lived through Jim Crow, the Klan, the founding of the NAACP, the Great Depression, the Harlem Renaissance, the Montgomery Bus Boycott, two World Wars, as well as the Civil Rights and Black Power movements, the Million Man and Million Woman marches and to see the first African American elected president of the United States. Their experiences have been varied, based on where they lived and learned in the United States, their education and socioeconomic status, cultural origins, religious affiliations and other environmental factors. All this has gifted them with a plethora of knowledge based on their lived experiences and their placement in society. Each one has much to offer new generations of black youth and families. They are living histories of our sojourn as a people in these United States. They have many stories waiting to be told, if only we would invite them to share. They have much to teach us, if we would become willing students. Their experience can be our support and our guide, if we would create the space for them to continue to learn and grow with us in the new millennium.

We have but to call them.

This guidebook is not meant to be an academic or intellectual exercise. It is a simple guidebook, designed for those interested in our continuance. In it you will find a model for community Councils of Elders, along with practical steps and processes for ways to engage our entire community in reconnecting the links that have historically been our strength. The guide also includes appendices of tools and processes to assist communities to plan, execute and move forward a process of developing a functional Council of Elders. This guidebook is your encouragement to make the call that could mean the difference between our annihilation or our continuation in strength, health and unity. It's in your hands. Will you make the call?

---

[2] Yeo G, Hikoyeda N, McBride, M, et al. Cohort Analysis as a Tool in Ethnogeriatrics: Historical Profiles of Elders from Eight Ethnic Populations in the United States. 2nd ed. Working Paper No. 12. Stanford, CA: Stanford Geriatric Education Center; 1998.

CHAPTER 1:
Getting Started: An Overview

Our Story

Several years ago in Wichita, Kansas the regional substance abuse prevention center in our area was struggling to figure out how to engage the black community in its substance abuse prevention efforts. To assist their work, they called together an advisory group of key leaders from the black community, including representatives from community-based organizations, human service professionals, public officials representing the community, community activists and organizers, and individuals who had previously demonstrated an interest in youth, families or community improvement. Over several months, the group met on a monthly basis, to talk about community issues, activities and initiatives designed to address some of those issues, and the difficulty of engaging community residents in efforts to address their own issues. Ultimately, it occurred to us that perhaps from our vantage point (primarily professionals serving a particular community), we weren't as clear as we needed to be about the true needs of the local residents and how best to meet them. We decided that it would make the most sense to ask those we hoped to effectively serve. Thus, we developed community input processes, surveys and focus groups to get a better idea of how our Council of caring professionals might best be of service in our community, particularly as it related to preventing youth from becoming involved in substance abuse.

What we found was that, although substance abuse was an issue, most of the locals we heard from understood that such abuse was more often a symptom of greater problems and issues that, if not dealt with, would only continue to manifest symptoms destructive to our community. They saw the rampant crime, drug use, and gang involvement as mere byproducts of poverty and economic distress which contributed to a weakened family and community structure, but also understood that the symptoms continued to feed the problem – often leading to broken families due to drug addiction, crime and imprisonment, poor academic progress and school dropout, and more. Respondents offered an array of ideas for addressing these issues, many of which had not been previously conceived of by our advisory group.

One such idea, that came up too often to be ignored, was the need to re-engage elder members of the community in whatever ways made the most sense. Residents spoke of the times when elders were more respected and revered. They talked about how important grandparents have always been in our community – the anchor of many extended family networks and the keeper of family histories and connections. They mentioned the need to have access to the years of wisdom they believed was a byproduct of having lived long, particularly as black men and women, and having been first-hand witnesses to the struggles that our community – the black community – has endured over the decades and centuries. More than a handful recognized the assets we had in our elders, but most also recognized the subtle change in our culture and the broader culture, which has begun to marginalize the elderly – to toss them aside after a certain age or life stage and no longer respect or revere them. Some were extremely concerned that many youth no longer respected adults in general, let alone the elderly among us. They saw re-engaging our elders as an important step toward achieving family strengthening and, ultimately, community revitalization.

The advisory group took the information from community members and contemplated the best way to respond to the data. The regional prevention center, whose role was primarily focused on substance abuse prevention education, allowed the community advisory group space and support to develop more comprehensive strategies to respond to the broader issues revealed through our community assessment processes. The idea to call the elders into service was one of those strategies. However, we understood that identifying and implementing a structure that would allow the elders to fully participate in ongoing community problem-solving was critical to the operational success of such a concept.

And thus we began. In truth, this remains a work-in-progress. Much of the information this guide provides has resulted from our "learn-as-you-go" process. Even as I write, our local Council of Elders is in the process of restructuring, much along the lines of the model presented in this work. After nearly ten years of working together, passions have cooled and participation is down. We are in the midst of processes to reinvigorate the Council and to assure that it remains engaged in meaningful work. We continue to learn, grow and develop means to fully engage and utilize our elders in ways that empower both them and the community. Nevertheless, we have identified a broad model of things that must be considered and implemented for the best possible success of an initiative of this kind. In this guide, we examine those ideas and concepts, and provide a promising approach for developing a Council of Elders in your community. What follows is a brief overview of the steps and considerations. The terms associated with many of the concepts are from key Bantu and other African languages. I include these because I am convinced of the importance of rooting this effort in these original African ideals and ways of living from which our communities have been birthed and sustained over time.

CHAPTER 2:
What are Elders Councils?

As we enter the new millennium, something remarkable is transpiring. Nelson Mandela, a hero to all for his sacrifice for the freedom of Africans in South Africa, has led a new charge: for the establishment of a global Council of Elders. Assisted by somewhat unlikely compatriots, British Rock Star Peter Gabriel has encouraged this new formation. "In traditional societies, the elders always had a role in conflict resolution, long-term thinking and applying wisdom wherever it was needed. We are moving to this global village and yet we don't have our global elders."[3]

"African society, for example," says Dr. Nana Apt of the University of Ghana "is very intergenerational. We don't have the automatic association that turns advanced age into a state of dependency or illness. Elders in African society take care of children just as parents do. They are the support of their families. There is no arbitrary cut-off of their active life."

Indeed, in traditional and contemporary African society, elders are respected and trusted for their roles as mediators, facilitators and repositories of the collective knowledge and wisdom that extends back generations. Historically, in decentralized and stateless political societies in Africa, which often consisted of collectives of villages and towns in close proximity, instead of chiefdoms and other political structures, communities were governed by Councils made up of elder members of the community. These Councils often were the ones that selected the chief, if there was one, and that chief was accountable to the entire community, under mandate of the Council of Elders.

---

[3] South Africa The Good News Newsletter http://www.sagoodnews.co.za/newsletter_archive/the_counsel_of_elders.html

Says Mark Gorman of Help Age International: "The so-called developing world has much to teach industrialized societies about the fast-emerging new intergenerational social structure. Mostly it has to do with respect. The industrialized countries have developed very damaging stereotypes about ageing that don't exist in developing world societies."

In contemporary Kenya, where the last Council of Elders presided in the 1950s, Kikuyu have called for a non-political Council of Elders as official leaders and spokespersons for the community. In order to insure that the voice of the Kikuyu community is heard, especially when it goes outside of the interest of political groups, it is believed that a Council of Elders will insure that community leadership has a place at the decision-making table, to make certain that those at the community level are not taken for granted or injured by decisions made without their interests in mind.

Speaking in relationship to social and restorative justice in Kenya, Oricho (2009) says: "I think that regarding the nature of leadership it is a society's right to take the means necessary to achieve the purpose for which it exists. This is justified by the lawfulness of society's goals and means to achieve justice. The Council of Elders kept community social structures strong with respect, trust and honesty and they showed wisdom, intelligence, seriousness and leadership."[4]

Schiele (2000) emphasizes the complex and polydeterministic ways that traditional African societies viewed human behavior and community responsiveness. "Government and individual responsibilities are considered to be obligations motivated less by self-interest…than by the interdependence of humans as interactive 'social' beings" (p. 41). This was supported by the belief of community members in the potential and proclivity of human beings to do good, in stark contradiction to mainstream social constructions that often label some as deviant, immoral, and unworthy. [5]

Why here, Why now?

As we conclude the first decade of a new millennium, the African American community remains stressed. In its State of Black America report, issued in March 2009, the Urban League indicated that Blacks remain twice as likely to be unemployed, three times more likely to live in poverty and more than six times as

---

[4] Oricho, Dennis Otieno (200) Understanding the traditional Council of Elders and restorative justice in conflict transformation http://www.sjweb.info/documents/sjs/pjnewarticles/103-1-06ENG.pdf

[5] Schiele, J. (2000). *Human services and the Afrocentric paradigm.* New York: Haworth Press.

---

likely to be imprisoned compared with whites, with the greatest inequality related to economics, followed by social justice, health and education. Such inequality represents continued challenges for black families and the communities where we are represented.

Freeman and Logan (2004)[6] identify a number of contemporary challenges that continue to affect all Black families, regardless of socio-economic status. Among those are the losses of important intergenerational support networks that have historically provided a sense of family and racial continuity. Along with those losses comes a lessening of the cultural value base and the traditions, beliefs, and language that have provided a connectedness across generations and socio-economic status. In addition, those losses continue to increase the risks for African American children and adults to fail academically, and to make poor decisions that are likely to lead to destructive outcomes individually and for the family and community. Freeman and Logan also cite the gradual erosion of the spiritual center that has sustained the African American family throughout time. Additionally, social classism and other within-group barriers as well as the dearth of culturally-viable resources for social, political, and economic development threaten the ability for ongoing cultural development and maintenance. All of these challenges further bear witness to the need for a community and societal response that acknowledges and builds upon that which has historically sustained the Black family and community.

---

[6] Freeman, E. M., & Logan, S. L. (2004). An analysis, integration and application of Africentric and strengths approaches to Black families and communities. In E. M. Freeman & S. L. Logan (Eds.), *Reconceptualizing the strengths and common heritage of Black families: Practice, research and policy issues* (pp. 25 - 40). Springfield, IL: Charles C. Thomas.

A Historical Model for Councils of Elders

Councils of Elders are a unique and historical human service construct. Councils of Elders have their historical roots in indigenous African communities which viewed the Elders as repositories of knowledge and wisdom, and more importantly, as the guardians and purveyors of a community's values, traditions, norms and interests. One such model exists with the Bantu peoples of Central West Africa, in the regions of Angola, Cabinda, Zaire and the Congo. The Bantu utilize several terms and proverbs to describe the purpose and responsibilities of such Councils, called by several names among the different language groups of the region. The Luba refer to these Councils as *Lubanza*; among the Swahili, it is known as *Baraza*; The Kongo call it *Mbongi*. The Mbongi is considered "the principal institution of decision making, of community order and of direction towards...the 'red symbol" of biological life and of growth, not only physically and spiritually, but political, economic and technological as well" (Fu-Kiau 2007, p. 45). It is believed that a community avoids disorder and destruction when it is "under the supervision and direction of leaders who possess authority deeply rooted within the people's common consent according to their concepts and their cultural values" (pg. 10).

Among the Bantu people, in practice the Mbongi takes responsibility for all social conflicts within the community, and for deliberating on social, political and economic basic needs of the entire community. "All problems in the community run toward the Mbongi" (Fu-Kaiu 2007, p. 3). In addition, the Mbongi sets the standard for community life. The Mbongi also serves as the "think-tank" for community issues and instructs the community on proper customs and behaviors. As in the example in the introduction, the Mbongi is responsible for gathering the community into alliances around mutual issues, and protects/shelters the community from problems, both internally and externally. The Mbongi not only brings community members together, but also collects, shares and interprets community experiences. The Mbongi is considered central to the community, and is egalitarian in providing every community member the right to participate in order "to be sensibilized by the past experience and foster the present and the future" (p. 6). The Mbongi shapes community life and leadership. That leadership consists of those who "possess leadership deeply rooted within the people's common consent according to their concepts and cultural values...based upon their own economic systems and upon their constitutions, whether written or not" (p. 10). Although headed by Elders, the Mbongi provides space for youth to gather and learn as well. The Mbongi is a system of organized self-help that finds its strength in Elder leadership and service.

Historical and Contemporary Self-Help in America

Since the arrival of enslaved Africans to the Americas, there has been active movement by Black people for ensuring the well-being of Black people. Arguably the history of ongoing uprising throughout the slavery period, as well as organized movements out of slavery via the freedom movements such as the Underground Railroad, mark a significant history of Black people helping each other to achieve a humane quality of life. The abolishment of the legal institution of slavery and the institutionalization of racism saw new institutions developed by Africans to more intentionally assist each other in the transition from slavery to freedom, based on a shared worldview colored by their relationship to a common history of oppression and marginalization. These new institutions came in the form of self-help, mutual aid organizations, and beneficence societies, early articulations of human service organizations, and were most prominent in the North as a response to the exodus of newly freed slaves from more overtly hostile southern states. These organizations sought, above all, to support individuals and families, for the strengthening of the whole community of Black people at all levels of society. As society has evolved, so have the issues that African Americans face and the helping organizations that serve African Americans. Historically, African American helping organizations have done the work of community and family strengthening with a particular focus on the development and well-being of African American children, working from a worldview that deems children's well-being as intricately tied to the wellness of their total environment.

African Americans have never been without organized social supports seeking to improve our lives and circumstances since our forced enslavement. Nevertheless, those efforts and organizations continue to change and redefine themselves as society and social policies impact their ability to support our core constituency. Post-emancipation, the migration of southern Blacks to northern regions of the United States increased the need for such supports in more direct and targeted ways. The majority of these efforts have been self-help initiatives of one sort or another. From the extended family and the Black church to mutual aid societies and benevolence organizations, post-emancipation Blacks have consistently managed to provide assistance to each other and to the community as a whole. Most such aid was localized and personal, emphasizing education, economic development, vocational training, culture, and social justice – all related to the strengthening and survival of the Black community. Self-help was and is one of the most common forms of social intervention focused on empowerment, and early human services efforts of African Americans were geared toward empowering individuals, families, and communities. Nevertheless, even when efforts were focused on individual-level interventions, such assistance was never seen as operating outside the focus on overall community development and strengthening. Individual "failure" was just as certainly "community failure," and as such, it was the community's responsibility to aid and assist individuals and families to overcome dire situations and circumstances. In large part, this was due to the belief and understanding that the dehumanizing effect of race and racial oppression significantly impacts, then and now, the life chances of people of African heritage in the United States.

The African American self-help and mutual aid movement proliferated in the North but existed throughout the continental United States. African Americans of all classes both assisted and were provided assistance through such avenues. The Black Women's Club movement of the late 1800s and early and mid-1900s had as their motto "Lifting as We Climb," declaring the belief and commitment to those of relative means to assist those with less to rise above socially imposed limitations, all for the good of the entire community and race. As a precursor to contemporary African American human service organizations, they were not exempt from viewing their work as moral work also; however, those values and morals were contextualized within a race-conscious agenda and worldview that unmistakably comprehended the limitations and exemptions of African Americans within mainstream social justice.

For African Americans, organized helping constructs, such as the Mbongi, or Councils of Elders, often form the vehicle for "Nia"[7] or the intentional/purposeful "doing." The very act of gathering and organizing resources in response to an identified need is an intention to impact a context or a system of contexts with the expectation of change. Beyond that, how those resources are selected, organized, and imbued with and generative of meaning represent the potential extension of intentionality, comprising a systematic mechanism for organizational and African American community efficacy. Organizations with adequate capacity to address the needs of African Americans may be those that couple creative leadership and empowering environments with meaningful and progressive technologies. The goal is to empower individuals, families, and communities to identify and name the nature of their struggles and to respond in ways that lead to a more equitable distribution of resources for family and community strengthening. Empowering practice increases what Freire (1970)[8] refers to as the "conscientization" of constituents, equipping them with definitions and tools to begin to ask generative questions thereby impacting change in themselves and within the environments where they exist. Thus, Councils of Elders represent both a connection/re-connection with historical practices that have proven empowering, as well as progressive and generative processes for community stability, wellness and growth. The Mbongi of West Africa provides a promising model. Throughout this guide, we'll be looking at what applications and modifications make sense to institute such Councils for contemporary diasporic African communities, particularly African American urban communities.

---

[7] A KiSwahili term meaning: "Purpose." The fifth principle of the Nguzo Saba as conceptualized by Dr. Maulana Karenga as the seven basic values of African culture.

[8] Freire, P. (1970). Pedagogy of the oppressed. New York: Continuum.

CHAPTER 3:
What is an Elder?

So, what is an elder or who qualifies to be an elder? Generally, an elder is one of advanced years, who is highly respected in her or his community of origin or residence. That respect is generated from their demonstration of sound character, good judgment and sensitivity to issues impacting their community. Most often, an elder has influence, within and beyond their immediate community and exhibits a willingness to speak out for the benefit and wellness of those who may have lesser voice.

Goggins (1998), in his exemplary guide on developing African centered rites of passage programs, explains that "Elders are the people who have the most invested in the village and therefore are most accountable." Writes Goggins: "Elders have the time to perfect living and gain wisdom. Eldership is a position earned by sharing what one has learned and accepting accountability for the growth and development of the village."[9]

The Eldership Project in Australia has made efforts to define the qualities that make up eldership.[10] These include:

LIFE
Their life experiences have led to deep learning.

GENEROSITY
They are willing and able to give of themselves.

---

[9] Goggins, L (1998) Bringing the light into a new day: African centered rites of passage. St. Rest Publications, Akron, OH
[10] http://www.eldership.com.au/about/qualities

ACCEPTANCE

They have come to accept life as it is, including their current condition, mistakes or injuries of the past and the insecurity of the future.

ACTIVITY

They are still active in life.

CONNECTION

They are connected to nature/spirit and to community.

FREEDOM

They have the freedom to speak their mind because they are no longer seeking to ascend in life and do not need to be concerned with the politics of success. They are also not attached to much.

COURAGE

They are willing to stand up and speak out. And they have the courage to face their own lives as is.

SELF-VALIDATION

They have a deep appreciation of their own self and while they may enjoy the validation of others, they do not seek it in the way younger men and women do. Their validation comes from the Spirit or from within.

JOI DE VIVRE

They have an easy joy for life.

PRIORITIES

They have developed a sense of what is – and is not – important.

CURIOSITY

They are still curious, still interested, still fascinated by life, still learning.

HOPE

Despite the darkness in the world or of their own life experience, they have hope.

CALMNESS

They are not afraid, not hassled, not rushed.

AWARENESS

They have developed a keen awareness of their own self (psyche, personality, mind, shadow, etc). They may not have a perfect or complete understanding, but they have dedicated themselves to self-awareness – to "KNOW THYSELF".

EMPATHY

They can sense and feel and understand the feelings of others.

COMPASSION

They are sensitive, forgiving and compassionate.

MORTALITY
They are aware of and actively developing a final relationship with dying. They can face death, eyes open. They can think and talk about it. It is safe to explore death in their presence – and develop a deeper appreciation of life.

LISTENING
They listen. Actively. Carefully. Lovingly. They know when to speak, when to ask questions and when to be silent.

SAFETY
They bring a spiritually grounded safety to relationships and interactions.

CONTEMPLATION
They relish and require silence and contemplation – as distinct from passivity, boredom or listless inaction.

ACTION
They know when to act or speak and their actions are grounded in that depth of contemplation.

RESOLUTION
They have mostly resolved the grievances, hurts, mistakes and lost opportunities of their lives. They are not still kicking themselves or mentally imprisoning others for the past. As well as they are able, they have learnt from those things, healed and left those things behind.

RESPECT
They respect others and are respected by others.

HEALING
They may be able to bring healing arts to new or old wounds.

ALCHEMY
They have the capacity to affect, influence or lead transformation in conflicts, situations or individuals.

GRACE
Hard to define. But true Elders have got it.

As we can ascertain from the previous list of attributes of an elder, it is obvious that simply being of adequate age (55 – 60+) does not necessarily qualify one to assume the important role of eldership. The Australian project goes on to identify some disqualifying factors that should be given serious consideration as a community develops their process of calling elders and establishing community Councils. Some individuals of advanced age may not be qualified to act as Elders if they:

- Have learnt little or nothing of wisdom.

- They are unwilling and unable to give of themselves.

- They deny life and cannot accept their past, present or future.

- They are passive and have no interest in ever being active again.

- They are disconnected from nature/spirit and/or the community (either by their own choice or by neglect or lack of opportunity).

- They are still seeking to ascend, win, inflate and puff themselves up and are – therefore – still attached to self-image and receiving the validation of others. They are, thus, not free to feel, think and speak authentically.

- They lack the courage to stand up and speak out.

- They have little joy for life.

- They still get caught up in life's petty quarrels or focus on things that are really not important.

- They are not curious or interested – they have stopped learning.

- They have no hope for the world.

- They are stressed, frazzled, hurrying, anxious.

- They have little or no self-awareness (generally characterized by such things as: offending others and never understanding why, being offended by others with no real understanding of why, only seeing other people's problems, always blaming others in conflict, taking no responsibility, etc).

- They cannot truly sense and feel and understand the feelings of others.

- They are insensitive, unforgiving and discompassionate. They are more likely to judge, blame and punish.

- They are unable or unwilling to look at dying. It is unsafe to discuss death in their presence.

- They do not listen.

- They don't know when to shut up.

- It might not be safe to be in their presence.

- They avoid silence and find contemplation meaningless or painful.

- They act without thinking.

- They still carry the grievances, hurts, mistakes and lost opportunities of their lives.

- They do not respect others and are probably not truly respected.

- They lack the gifts of healing.

- They lack the capacity to affect, influence or lead genuine, positive transformation in conflicts, situations or individuals.

- They have no interest in ever becoming an Elder.

Age Eligibility

It is up to each individual community to decide the age criteria for members of its Council of Elders. In our community, we set the age at 60 and over. One reason for this is that most individuals in contemporary society don't reach retirement age until 65, or occasionally at 62. Setting the age minimum at 60 allows us to tap elders who may be still engaged in professional work, and thus are still linked to networks that prove helpful in supporting Council work. We potentially catch them before they leave the world of former work, which allows them to make those connections which may remain after their retirement.

However, we also have a graduated membership structure that includes all age groups. Other membership categories include the following, all of which are considered *Scribes* (see Chapter 10: Council Structure for more information):
1) 50 to 59- Associate Elders
2) 18 to 49- Warriors/Nation Builders/Apprentices
3) 3 to 17- Infusion Stages
4) Birth to 2- Modeling Stages

Are there elders in your community who meet these criteria? No doubt there are a number of them. In moving forward to intentionally establish a local Council of Elders, then, the first step is to identify them. Nevertheless, it is important that a foundation is laid in anticipation of calling them forth that honors who they are, what they've done, and your hopes for their assistance in the future life of the community.

CHAPTER 4:
The Planning Group

After years of doing organizational development work with community-based nonprofit and grassroots organizations, I have ascertained that a major challenge that many start-up organizations face is the lack of broad-based support for their efforts. Most often, an organization founder has determined a need within the community, and has fashioned, often in isolation, what they feel is an appropriate response for that need. With all the best intentions, the founder will set out to establish an organization that will serve the identified clientele or address the need. Finding resources to accomplish the organization's goal is always an issue; thus, most founders determine that they must become a federally-recognized tax-exempt nonprofit, and thus make efforts to become established as such, complete with "board of directors" and a set of articles and bylaws. And thus they begin.

There are several problems with this approach, but for the purpose of this guide, I want to focus on a potentially problematic initial premise that can create increased challenges as the organization continues through its lifecycle. In particular, for the development of a community-based Council of Elders, although one person or a few core people may have initially made the decision to pursue the possibility of developing such a Council, a successful Council will require significant community engagement from the very beginning.

Development of a community Council of Elders, in order to insure success, must be a cogent response to a real or perceived community need. How that need is expressed may be different from one community to the other. For example, in our community, the results of an extensive community needs assessment led to the development of a comprehensive response to community needs related to substance abuse prevention, one of which was the Council of Elders. In another community where a Council has been established, community residents were responding to the academic achievement gap of black students in the public school system. As a result, many of their original elders were retired educators. That is not to suggest that the Council should ever be limited to elders in particular professions or with particular interests; however, the needs of the community being served must be both the impetus and the guide for how the Council ultimately develops. In addition, later I will discuss a recommended Council structure, based on the Mbongi, which will further clarify the need for diversity on the Council.

In order for the proposed work to be truly responsive to actual community issues, it will be important early on to involve as planners a group of collaborators connected to the community in a variety of ways. This need not be a large group, but it will help if they are representative of the community, including being intergenerational.

The work of this planning group is obviously to plan. But their role is not to endeavor to set up the Council on their own. Theirs is to begin to assess the needs and interests of the community as it relates to engaging seniors in its ongoing development. While it may require extensive information gathering, it is not necessarily required that the group engage in a complex and extensive surveying process. It is quite possible that there is already some information available from data collection performed by other entities serving the community. This might include the school district, social service agencies and other service providers who are engaged in various activities directed toward the community. For example, if the school district has data that indicates achievement disparities, there may be groups in the community who are attempting to address this issue, and in the process have conducted further needs assessment to look at reasons why this is a problem. Consequently, the information they have been able to ascertain can provide some basis for the call you will ultimately make to the community at large to mobilize them around the issues that have been identified, and to gather consensus about the desire for engaging community elders to assist with efforts to address relevant issues.

Another responsible that this planning group may take on, once enough data has been gathered to justify the need and desire for a Council of Elders, is to begin developing a governance framework. This construction need not be so rigidly defined that once the Council is established, it dictates how they will govern themselves. But it does need to address how the community will determine the

Council's vision and mission, and ultimately how it will "call" the elders to request their involvement. This will be discussed more in the next chapter.

Finally, and most importantly, the planning group will need to clearly define the "who, what, why, when and where" for next steps. Who, in this case, relates to which stakeholders need to be involved in the next phase of planning for the potential calling forth and development of the Council. Again, the goal is broad-based consensus from members of the community being served. Next to be decided is the type of forum where key stakeholders will be called together for discussion. It will be important to structure that discussion, which may be a one-time gathering, or an ongoing conversation, so that everyone involved feels that their input is valued and important.

Often, in communities, some voices are "louder" than others, based on age, occupation, or other perceived value within the community. Youth, for instance, sometimes feel their opinion is drowned out by the adults of the community; unemployed or non-professional members of the community may feel their opinions carry less weight than professional or "accomplished" members of the community. One of the planning group's greatest challenges will be designing an input process that is as egalitarian as possible, where everyone who is interested has the opportunity to be heard and their input valued.

Consideration needs to be given to logistics like time, location, wording of the invitation, etc. so that stakeholders have the sense that they are a very integral part of a making decisions that will impact their community. For example, if you really want to hear from youth, a gathering time will need to be set when they are available, e.g. not during school hours. The structure of the gathering, too, requires forethought and consideration. Oftentimes, when the community is called together around issues, especially critical issues that may carry strong emotions and concerns, such gatherings can become hours-long gripe sessions, where attendees utilize such a forum to focus on the myriad problems and examples of the problems, leaving little time for solution development. You don't want this to be that gathering, and thus, your advanced planning of the structure and format will be crucial in keeping participants focused and engaged on the development of a Council of Elders as a potential solution. The next chapter will also outline some possible tools and processes that can assist in that effort.

CHAPTER 5:
Assessing Community Readiness and Building Support

One of the planning group's primary activities is gathering information to support the desire for a community Council of Elders. In the previous chapter, we talked about gathering available data about the issues facing the community. The next critical step is hearing directly from the community about what they perceive as key issues and concerns. There are several ways to get to this information, including surveying, focus groups, community forums, etc. The method you choose should be based on your knowledge of the community and the best way to reach those you feel will provide the most useful information, being conscious, as previously mentioned, to include as broad a base of input as possible. A recent publication offered free online by Promotions West, *Outreach to African Americans,* provides several good strategies for reaching the community.[11] One strategy they recommend is to survey the community.

As a first step, the steering committee will need to determine what it wants to know from the community. It could be as simple as a few questions asking about community members' knowledge of Councils of Elders, their interest in having one in their community, and how they feel such a Council might be utilized. Or, it could be much more comprehensive, based on other preliminary data-gathering, and

---

[11] Wagner, Michael (2009) *Outreach to African Americans.* Promotions West.
http://promotionswest.com/Welcome_files/Outreach_to_African_Americans.pdf

focused on prioritizing community issues that residents feel are most salient and requiring the most immediate attention. What you decide you need most to hear about from the community will have some bearing on the next step.

The next step is to determine what makes sense in terms of survey creation and administration for your community. It is not necessary that this be an empirically sound, random selection-type survey, although depending on who is helping with this initial planning it could be fairly comprehensive. For example, if you have college students or professors as part of your steering committee, it may be possible that survey development and administration can be formulated as a course project. You just want to hear from an assortment of people. So, what is the best way to gather that information, utilizing a survey? It may be that you decide to do a phone survey, based on community zip codes, utilizing your local phone directory. In this instance, you would need to consider that many people either have unlisted phone numbers or rely solely on cell phones that are usually not listed in local directories either. Thus, your responses run the risk of being severely limited and possibly skewed. Are there upcoming or regular community gatherings, such as fairs or festivals, where you can gather information from many people in one setting? Are there local venues where many in the community often or regularly visit over time, such as community centers or grocery stores? You may be able to set up booths for information collection at these events or venues over a period of time, to solicit information from residents. Even local school enrollment time offer opportunities to come in contact with neighborhood parents, who invariably have opinions, ideas and valuable input for your efforts. Other possible venues may include:

- Laundromats
- Barber shops
- Health clinics
- Shopping malls
- Churches (of course)
- Public housing
- College campuses
- Book stores
- Theaters
- Community-based organizations serving African Americans

Maybe you'll decide a survey is not the best route. Perhaps you'd rather talk one-on-one with community members, or talk with them in small groups to discuss their concerns and interests. Many of the aforementioned information sources can be equally helpful utilizing either of these methods.

However you decide to solicit input, the goal is to hear from as many people as possible to generate both information (for the steering committee) and interest (from the community) about your plans to establish a Council of Elders, and what the community feels will be the most important role(s) for such a Council. After the information is gathered and analyzed, you'll have information to ground the next steps of the process. In addition, the process of gathering information itself will lay the groundwork for the next step: building community support.

Analyzing the Data – Developing Preliminary Value Statements

Some of the information that you will be looking for in all the data gathered is a sense of what the community feels are the most pressing issues it is facing. However, in addition to that, you will want to begin interpreting community values represented by those issues. Oricho speaks of keeping "community social structures strong with respect, trust and honesty…wisdom, intelligence, seriousness and leadership" as well as forgiveness, healing, empowerment and encouragement. In the Congo nations referred to by Fa-Kaiu, the Mbongi or Council ideally represents, inculcates and upholds the "concepts and values based upon their own economic systems and upon their constitution, written or not. It is here that the African modern [Council] should find its true source of inspiration and revival" (pg. 10). In reality, most urban African American communities are suffering from the lack of such a constitution, written or not, and find ourselves increasingly moving away from even the most basic of community values recognized and supported by our ancestors, pre- and post-enslavement. One reason may be the lack of a clear articulation of those values, customs, traditions and norms that have historically provided for our survival in the United States. Although many among us still hold these values as important, indeed critical, more often than not, the inability to coalesce around them is hampered by our failure to clearly identify and articulate them, and then to find common ground and impetus to promote and enforce them.

Our Council of Elders, when it was originally instituted, decided to use the Nguzo Saba as it value system. The Nguzo Saba was first created and articulated as part of the celebration of Kwanzaa, a uniquely African American holiday created by Maulana Ron Karenga and the Us Organization in the late 1960s. The Nguzo Saba value system includes seven key social and spiritual principles believed by the organization, and since then, communities of African descended people, to be the basic grounding for community unity, empowerment and progress. Those values are:

1. **UMOJA** (UNITY) (oo-MOE-jah) - To strive for and maintain unity in the family, community, nation and race.

2. **KUJICHAGULIA** (SELF DETERMINATION) (koo-jee-cha-goo-LEE-ah) - To define ourselves, name ourselves, create for ourselves and speak for ourselves.

3. **UJIMA** (COLLECTIVE WORK AND RESPONSIBILITY) (oo-JEE-mah) - To build and maintain our community together and to make our brothers' and sisters' problems our problems and to solve them together.

4. **UJAMAA** (COOPERATIVE ECONOMICS) (oo-JAH-mah) - To build and maintain our own stores, shops and other businesses and to profit together from them.

5. **NIA** (PURPOSE) (nee-AH) - To make as our collective vocation the building and developing of our community in order to restore our people to their traditional greatness.

6. **KUUMBA** (CREATIVITY) (koo-OOM-bah) - To do always as much as we can, in the way that we can, in order to leave our community more beautiful and beneficial than when we inherited it.

7. **IMANI** (FAITH) (ee-MAH-nee) - To believe with all our hearts in our parents, our teachers, our leaders, our people and the righteousness and victory of our struggle.

Another value orientation that may be useful as a starting point for developing a community-based value system and guiding principles are the principles of Ma'at. Ma'at is an ancient Egyptian concept, personified by the goddess of the same name. Ma'at represents Truth, Justice, Balance and Order. More than a deity, Ma'at was the personification of Universal Order, underlying everything else. Those principles are: ***Truth, Justice, Harmony, Balance, Order, Reciprocity and Propriety***.

The data collected as part of your readiness process can and should be the beginning of clearly identifying and codifying such values. Although the query can be direct to those who are responsive to our questions (e.g. "What are the values you feel make for a strong community?"), we will also need to look beneath the surface of the issues that surface, to drill down to the underlying values represented by the problems and concerns that are articulated. For example, if a recurring theme is lack of employment for youth, some of the underlying values may be community economic sufficiency and meaningful rites of passage for youth into responsible adulthood. Thus, the interpretation of the data is critical in beginning the process of clearly identifying and articulating those important community values, customs and traditions, whether they are currently practiced or not. The themes garnered through this interpretive process will be presented later as you begin to develop preliminary purposes and mission for the Council.

CHAPTER 6:
Developing Purpose and Mission

Based on the information gathered from community input processes, the steering committee should have at least a general idea of how the community feels a Council of Elders might benefit the community. From that, the steering committee will need to develop a purpose statement and a focused mission for the Council of Elders. Purpose, or the vision statement, defines an overall idea of how the community will be changed/better because the Council exists and based on a timeline in the distant but foreseeable future. That future could be five years, ten years, or twenty years out. It is important, though, that there is a predetermined point at which you would expect to see noticeable impact, and what that impact will be should be succinctly described in your purpose statement. The purpose statement should be inspiring, and should energize both your planning group, and ultimately the gathering of elders and the community they will serve. Your purpose statement is not your mission statement. We'll talk more about that later. However, a good purpose or vision statement will assist you in formulating the Council's mission, as they are complementary in nature.

A Council's mission statement clearly outlines the prime purposes of the work of the Council, including clearly identified markers and measures of success. The mission statement is both a declaration to those internal to the Council, as well as those without, to keep the Council on point as to what it hopes to achieve by any and all activities in which it engages.

The vision statement is equally important, but is more overarching, defining and declaring the operational values and guiding assumptions and beliefs that give impetus to the Council's very existence. For the Council itself, it provides inspiration and motivation, as well as expressing expectations for how everyone involved will behave and perform to exemplify the Council's highest standards. For those external to the Council, it provides a rationale for partnership and collaboration, based on mutual agreed-upon beliefs and values. Here is where community values exposed through the data gathering process are critical.

Your Statement of Purpose

The purpose statement should be developed first, and should be expressed in powerful phrasing that encapsulates the Council's reason for being. The vision or Statement of Purpose, then, should declare its goal of delivering or assisting the deliverance of the best possible outcome. Keep in mind, that outcome needs to correlate strongly with what has been heard from the community, particularly the common values that have been suggested or explicitly expressed.

A process to help define what that vision will be is to theme the input received from the community. Are there particular areas of concern or interest that continued to come up from community members? What did you hear related to their perception of the current state of affairs versus a "better" state of affairs?

In addition, the planning group will want to take time to clarify its own values, assumptions and guiding principles. This will not necessarily be easy work. In any group, there will be differences in all of these areas. It is critical that the group take the necessary time to work through these and come up with a core inventory of values and guiding principles that ALL can agree on. Ultimately, these will represent the community "constitution," if you will, that will guide all of the work of the Council. It may be helpful to enlist a skilled, outside facilitator to help with this process. However, the appendices include activities and tools that can assist you in this process.

Once that is accomplished, the group will be in the best position to begin crafting its Statement of Purpose. Again, a good Statement of Purpose clearly articulates the broad vision and aspirations for the Council. For example:

"Believing in the value and worth of every human being, and believing that African people worldwide and within individual communities throughout the world have many gifts to share among ourselves and with the world, the vision of the African American Council of Elders is to…."

Your Statement of Purpose, unlike a Mission Statement, can be as long as it need be to clearly articulate who you are, your values and guiding principles, and why you exist. You want to create a vision in the minds of those who read or hear it that energizes and inspires them to want to know more, be more or do more, in relationship to your work. It's all about inspiration!

Your Statement of Purpose should speak to the best possible outcome(s) for the work in which the Council is engaged. It should speak to how the world would/will be different if you are successful in your mission and endeavors. It should serve as your "North Star," the "promised land" that you will inhabit if your keep moving in the direction of your ambitions.

Your Statement of Purpose shouldn't include measurable objectives or concretized outcomes. That is the work of your Mission Statement and the goals and outcome projections that will ultimately be developed from your Mission Statement.

The purpose statement should be powerful and compelling, inspiring creativity, originality and quality. It should move you past what is and toward all that is possible. Of course, it should be realistic; while at the same time moving you outside of the box of what is common and easy. It may not be realistic to say: "We envision a world where all children can fly." However, the idea of a world where all children can live and develop up to the fullness of their individual potential is infinitely doable, given the right circumstances, if your mission is to create those circumstances.

In the words of Albert Einstein: "Imagination is more powerful than knowledge." Your Purpose Statement should trigger the imagination, and point toward the greatest of possibilities. It should energize the passions of those who are involved or who you want to involve.

Other Purpose Statement tips:

- It should be written in present tense, describing what you anticipate actually seeing, hearing, feeling and thinking when your vision is realized.

- It should inspire the emotions and passions of those hearing it.

- It should include sensory details – colors, sounds, scenes, shapes and images.

The Mission Statement for the Council of Elders

Similar to the Vision or Purpose Statement, the Mission Statement of an organization or group gathered for collective work informs the group's members and supporters of its overall goal and purpose. However, it is different from a vision or purpose in that it gives more specific guidance about the actual work in which the group will be engaged. For example, a group may have as its vision that "all children and families will experience the highest quality of life possible, as it relates to health, education and general welfare…." Subsequently, the group's mission may be more specific, declaring that its particular work is to "act as an educational resource and support to youth and families related to the history and culture of the African Diaspora in order to create pride in heritage and a commitment to ongoing achievement."

The mission represents why the Council exists currently. The mission should be succinct, such that each member of the Council is able to verbally express it. To help the Council to ground its mission, it's important to ask two questions: "What aspirations does the Council have for the world in which it operates and has some influence over?", and "What can/does the Council do or contribute to fulfill those aspirations?"

An effective mission should:
- Define what the Council does
- Define what the Council aspires to be
- Limit the work of the Council, to exclude some ventures
- Be broad enough to allow for creative growth
- Distinguish the Council from other Councils
- Serve as a framework to evaluate the Council's current activities
- Be clearly stated so that it can be understood by all

An easy exercise to begin the process of defining the Council's mission is to answer these three critical questions: "Our Council does/will do [what?] for [whom?] so that [What?]." The "what" represents the general work of the Council, for example: "The Council of Elders provides culturally specific academic guidance and support…." The "who" tells members and supporters who the Council will serve, for example: "The Council of Elders provides culturally specific academic guidance and support to youth and families in Camden's community of African-descended residents…." Answering the question, "so that" is an important one. It provides the basis for the broad and overall evaluation of the Council's effort. "The Council of Elders provides culturally specific academic guidance and support to youth and families in Camden's community of African-descended residents, so that youth and families aspire to excellence and achievement in all of their endeavors." Ultimately, you will need to refine the words until you have a concise and precise statement of your mission, which expresses your ideas, measures and desired result.

Once the planning group has adequately defined its purpose (vision) and mission, you are ready to move to the next step: making the "Call," or inviting your particular community/village to identify elders worthy of the call to Elderhood.

CHAPTER 7:
Making the "Call" and Inviting the Elders

In the community where I live, our process was initiated by the community expressing a desire to return our elders to their traditional stature of respect and role of wisdom-providers. We chose to elevate that desire to a mandate for action and began the process by turning back to the community to ask them what they thought would be qualifications for a representative body of individuals who might constitute a Council. Based on those qualifications (most of which are outlined in Chapter 3: What is an Elder?), we developed a nomination process, whereby community members could identify and invite esteemed elder members of the community to be seated in this capacity.

The process included nomination forms, which included biographical information and a statement from the identified individual that they would be willing to act as a community elder on the Council. Because we were not working from any pre-existing template, we had to create our own, unique to our community. Nevertheless, after nine years of working with the Council, we've determined that there is some basic information that would be helpful for the community and potential elders to consider as part of the call to Elderhood. In the appendix, you will find a basic "nomination form" that you can use or modify for your particular community.

Critical to this process, however, is getting the word out broadly so that your Council is populated with a truly representative body of individuals. Our community is strongly church-focused; however, the planning group wanted to make sure that individuals from diverse faith traditions and those who were not affiliated with any religious group were included on the Council. As a note, although the

Council is not linked to any particular religious tradition (e.g. Christianity or Islam), community members and the planning group did feel that it was important that potential Council candidates did find a role for spirituality in their lives.

Through the previous processes of consulting the community, the planning group will have piqued interest and, hopefully, some level of buy-in from the community. No doubt, as the idea has been floated about the desire for and possibility of an Elders Council, many individuals have begun thinking of individuals they feel would be suitable for such a Council. At this phase in the process, these are the individuals to whom you will return to request their assistance in garnering nominations for a Council. In addition, any available community communication networks should be utilized to get the word out.

In the meantime, the planning group needs to determine how many elders it feels are needed to represent the community. This determination will be different from community to community, and based on the vision and mission the group has determined for itself. For example, if the group has decided its mission is primarily related to academic achievement, it will then need to identify the important and specific spheres of influence that can impact this mission. It may decide that educators, parents/grandparents, clergy, and individuals in other professions will provide a well-rounded selection of knowledge, skills, experience and ability. It is my suggestion that the size of the Council only be limited by the number of individuals willing to actively participate. As you will see in the chapter on suggested structure, there is a potential role for all.

Next, the planning group will need to determine what information it needs to gather about potential elders, in order to make sure there is a suitable pool of candidates nominated and willing to serve. Although it is important not to have such a large Council that it becomes difficult to manage, I would encourage that the "qualifications" be basic enough so that any willing elder who is nominated has the opportunity to serve. What you will find is that not all who are nominated will be willing to take on the task, and even some of those who initially agree to serve may find that they don't desire to continue, for whatever reason. Nevertheless, those basic qualifications need to encompass those things that have been deemed important by the community, based on your previous information-gathering work. For example, if the community has expressed the desire to have individuals who have exhibited/demonstrated some level of service to the community, you will want to have that as criteria. How that service has been demonstrated may be variable – it could mean providing something as informal as provided oversight to youth and families on a neighborhood block, to serving in the public sphere in a more formal role. Your nomination process should allow for the nominators to describe what that service has been. I've included a sample "nomination questionnaire" in the appendix. One thing you will probably want to encourage nominators to have is the expressed willingness of the nominee to serve. In order to insure this, you will need to prepare and disseminate a description of what you envision for the Council, even if it is just basic information that tells the "what" and "why" of what you're trying to accomplish. A "role description" is imperative. Individuals who are approached about the possibility of serving should have as much information as is available about what they are being asked to participate in.

As noted, the size of the Council may vary. In fact, modeling after the structure of the Mbongi, there may be members who serve on Council issue-centered "commissions" which may be implemented on a temporary, as-needed basis. (More about Council structure and commissions will be provided later.) Consequently, the more nominees the better. Also, the "call" is not a "one-time and forevermore" invitation. As the Council becomes established and new community members "age into" qualifications, you will be required to call again and/or seat new members.

The next step is to determine how the nomination process will be executed. Will you have paper nomination forms? An online process, e.g. simple e-mail or a more complex online application/nomination process? It might be appropriate to have several mechanisms for receiving nominations.   Not all individuals and families have access to technology so, although receiving nominations via technology generated sources can be easier to handle, the goal is to make the process easy and accessible to any and all who have interest in the development of the Council. It is important not to skew the process in a way that only a certain segment of the community can participate, e.g. the professional class. In fact, if the Council is to ultimately be successful, meaningful and respected, it must, above all things, be representative. Decide on a deadline for nominees, based on a predetermined timeline.

Once all the nominations have been received, you will need to develop a process for determining which elders to invite. Ideally and initially, I would encourage inviting them all, since your first engagement with them will be some type of orientation. At the orientation, they will have the opportunity to decide if serving on the Council is something they want to and are able to do. There will be some who opt out, for a variety of reasons, from poor health to simple disinterest. It might be good to promise (and provide) others opportunities for them to serve, as they are willing and able. At the very least, all of those nominated and oriented should be include on a contact list, to keep them informed about the activities of the Council. At some future date, they may decide they would like to become more involved.

CHAPTER 8:
The Orientation

The orientation for the Council will be the first opportunity to really spell out to potential Council members the values and guiding principles communicated via the community input process upon which the Council is being founded, and what the community desires of them. It is also an opportunity to find out what experience, skills, abilities, knowledge, and wisdom each of the potential Council members feel they have to offer and would be willing to share in service to the community. Likewise, it can provide the opportunity for the community to share what they can and would be willing to share with the elders, for their service. One good way to do this is through a GawaKazi process. Gawa is a KiSwahili term meaning "*to share*" and Kazi means "*work*." There will be more on that later.

At the very least, the orientation should include the following elements:
1. An icebreaker/introductions time;
2. Background and history of Elders Councils, in general, and the work-to-date toward a local Elders Council;
3. Review of vision and mission, as determined by planning group, with the caveat that once a Council is seated, they will be able to revise the particulars of the mission as they feel appropriate;
4. Brainstorming by the group about what activities make sense for their group to pursue in order to fulfill the vision and mission;
5. An opportunity for each individual in the group to reflect on their own personal mission and how that mission might fit within the context of the Council;

6. An opportunity for those individuals who feel ready and able to express personal commitments to the Council and the community (potentially committing to a "GawaKazi share");
7. Discussion on ways to maintain ongoing communication to the group; and
8. Information about the enstooling process.

The appendix includes a sample orientation agenda with activities for achieving all of these elements.

GawaKazi or Shared Work

An additional element that might be added to the orientation is the introduction to GawaKazi. GawaKazi is a practice that the Council, once it is formed, may desire to institute on a community-wide basis, as another way of contributing in a tangible manner to the community.

GawaKazi is a unique community value-exchange enterprise which honors the unique gifts, talents and resources of all members of the community and provides the opportunity to share those gifts, talents and resources. It is particularly appropriate as an initiative for an Elders Council, as it allows them and the community to place value of their offerings, as well as provides an opportunity for intergenerational sharing. The sharing can include things such as tutoring, yard work, simple repairs, running errands, and storytelling. However, it is only limited by the human resources available within the community. GawaKazi is based on values that are in synch with the values inherent in the concept of Elders Councils.

1. All members of the community are assets and have something to contribute.
2. Work is redefined to include any and all things that contribute to the overall health and wellbeing of the entire community.
3. Reciprocity is a community value that stresses "how can we help each other" versus "what do I get out of it?"
4. A network of people in any community working together is stronger and can achieve more than any one individual working alone.
5. Every human being matters, and should be treated with respect and dignity.

As part of the orientation, these values can be expressed and demonstrated. This requires that individuals from the community be willing to offer something to the elders at the same time that the elders make commitment offers. Thus, one of the orientation activities might include having each individual identify personal gifts and/or experience and make the commitment. See appendix for more information on GawaKazi.

Finally, make sure to allow plenty of time and space for questions, answers and discussion. Remember that the Council is (and should always be) a "work-in-progress" and you will want to continue to receive input, feedback, ideas and suggestions from the entire community. Also, make sure that you have the contact information for all interested elders, for follow-up and updates on the progress of the work.

CHAPTER 9:
Enstoolment: Celebration, Ritual and Pageantry

Once the members for the Council of Elders have been selected (through the nomination, invitation and self-selection process), it is good to plan for a community-wide "enstoolment" ceremony. It is good to have already established and considered a potential date for this ceremony at the time of the orientation, so that participants in the orientation can begin to plan accordingly.

While there is no standard ceremony for this process, there are several elements that you will want to be sure to include:

- Prayer (non-denominational)
- Libation Statement and Pouring of Libations (See appendix for sample libation statements)
- Explanation (historical background of Councils of elders and your community initiative)
- Youth
- Music (preferably African and especially African drumming)
- African Dance
- African-centered decoration
- Food

(See Appendix for sample Enstoolment agenda and script.)

The seating of the Council of Elders should provide an opportunity for the community as a whole to be re-introduced to the concept of Elders Councils, as well as to introduce those elders who are making a commitment to serve them. The vision and mission should be clearly spelled out, and ideally, be provided in written format. It should be a tasteful and celebratory occasion. Youth involvement should be encouraged, whether in some aspect of the ceremony itself, or through some mechanism that allows elders and youth to interact. The ceremony should include an opportunity for elders to make a public declaration of their commitment to serve. It should be made clear that the Council sits at the behest of the community and is thus accountable to the community, and likewise, the community is accountable to the Council. Finally, some type of "official" ornamentation should be bestowed upon the elders, designating them as the Council. In our community, Elders receive a Kente strip with "Council of Elders" embroidered into it.

CHAPTER 10:
The Work of the Council

Once the Council has been seated, the real work begins. Several first steps need to be accomplished. These include:

- Review of the Council's vision and mission.
- Development of an internal Council governance structure (a model/suggested structure will follow)
- Decision regarding whether Council will become a federally designated not-for-profit organization, if not already designated during the planning process. (Pros and cons of such a designation are included in the Appendix.)
- Development of concrete initial objectives
- Identification of strategic action steps to achieve the objectives, including necessary resources, as appropriate
- Development of a timeline for meeting objectives
- Development of a mechanism for consistent and ongoing communication between the Council and the community

The appendix includes tools to assist with this initial work.

Suggested Council Structure

Formal Western-style organizations typically have a basic governance structure that may include a President/Chair, Vice Chair, Secretary, Treasurer, etc. These are important organizational roles, as they help to facilitate the work and functioning of the organization. However, a Council of Elders is not a "typical" organization. First of all, the real "board of directors" for the organization is the community being served. The Council serves at their pleasure. This common organizational structure has the potential to make the Council too insular and removed from the actual work that it is to engage in: representing, advancing and upholding the community's "constitution." Thus, a potentially better structure for facilitating that work can be modified model of the Mbongi of Western Africa.

"The Mbongi, as the principal institution of the community, possesses its own leaders and their assistants to take care of the community's…diverse responsibilities". It should be noted that in the traditional African model, membership and certain roles are dictated by connection to a particular family or lineage. As such, some roles on the Mbongi do not translate for our purposes, as most community Councils will not be structured in this fashion (e.g. every Elder represents their own family, clan and/or lineage). It should also be noted, however, that undoubtedly each member of the Council WILL be connected to a particular family in the community, and as such, their first line of representation and governance is over their own family for, as a popular Ghanaian proverb so aptly states: *The ruin of a nation begins in the homes of its people."* Likewise, the building of any strong community must begin there, as well, and who better to institute positive forward movement than the Elders? Nevertheless, the Council roles described here are adaptations of those roles typical of a West African Mbongi, as described by Fu-Kiau.

Presiding Elder

At the head of this institution is the *"Mfumu-mbongi"* or Presiding Elder or Chief, who is "the well-known person of the institution and the most public figure…but he is not the 'person-pillar'" (Fu-Kiau 2007, pg. 21). The "person-pillars" are the "commissions." This individual serves as the public representative and symbolic head and spokesperson for the overall Council, although he only speaks at the behest of the community – he "blows the horn to gather its members. [However], as the horn of the community, he does not speak unless the community speaks through him" (pg. 22). His other roles include maintaining order within the proceedings of the Council, assigning and dispatching the Commissions, and directing the discussions and work of the Council.

Emissaries (N'swamis and N'kengi)

In this role, members act as what Fa-Kiau terms as *N'swamis* or *spies*, whose role it is to act as "watchmen, investigators and detectives" and "collect information…according to their professional particularities," as discreetly as necessary, to bring back to the Commission. These are not tasked to "spy" in the sense of covert operatives, so much as to pay attention and to engage the community in conversations regarding current conditions and aspirations for the future. They are specialists in specific areas, whose job it is to collect information from the community beyond the Council related to specific issues, to bring that information back into the Council circle for interpretation and discussion, and to make recommendations to the Council regarding the need for Commissions or further deliberation.   They are listeners. As "watchmen (*N'kengi*)," these individuals are also responsible for keeping close watch on the community and community members' behavior, concerns, and challenges among themselves and for the wellbeing of the community. ***The emissaries are responsible for encouraging community members directly impacted by an issue to bring their issue before the Council. It is important that issues before the Council HAVE BEEN INITIATED BY COMMUNITY MEMBERS WHO ARE NOT COUNCIL MEMBERS.***

These ***emissaries*** may then be called upon to serve on Commissions, based on their areas of specialization.

Commissions (Commissioners/Counselors)

Council Commissions are issue-focused groups, delegated by the Presiding Elder, that act as connectors to the internal and external stakeholders of the community. The commissions (and commissioners/Councilors) are central to the work of the Council. Areas in which Commissions may work include such focuses as: justice, education, economics, health, arts and cultural creation, politics and legislation, and Council maintenance. For this reason, it is important to have a diversity of specialization represented on the Council. In addition, other members of the community can (and should, where warranted) be included in the work of the Commission.

Commissions need not act as "standing committees (although they may)," but rather, should be launched based on issues brought before the Council as a whole. The Commission, once launched, is then responsible for gathering information, sponsoring debate within its group, making deliberations and crafting recommendations, based on its findings, and presenting these recommendations back to the larger Council. The Commission is responsible for selecting a spokesperson (Nzonzi), to present its findings.

*** The commissions may also call upon others in the community, who are not sitting Elders, to assist with commission work. This may be a good role

for Associate Elders, and/or the opportunity to engage those at the Associate Elder age level in Council work and beginning their mentoring process for ultimately becoming full Elders.

Commission Spokespersons (Nzonzi)

The individual selected for this role should exemplify wisdom, and understanding of and skills related to "matters and questions of justice, decision-making, negotiation, law, punishment, counseling" and conflict-resolution (pg. 25). She or he should also be skillful in finding and discerning truth and in communicating to individuals at any station in society. He or she is responsible for collecting everything that is discussed, both in Commissions and the Council as a whole, and to interpret and present the findings and recommendations of the represented Commission. The Spokesperson may also be called upon to present Council decisions to the larger community.

It should be noted here that no decisions of the Council can be binding and executed without the approval of the community. If the community determines that the Council has not brought forth a decision or determination which is executable, they may ask the Council to resume its deliberation.

Archivist (*Na-Makolo*)

The archivist is the information keeper for the Council. This person is responsible for keeping a record of all of the deliberations of the Council, and most importantly, its decisions and rulings. He or she is also responsible for keeping a record of all Council history.

Scribes

Although not included in the Bantu conceptualization of the Mbongi, our local Council has, since its beginning, included a class of members who are not age-eligible for Eldership, but who desire to provide support for the work of the Council. These individuals often act as assistants to Council members, and within the structured outlined here, might assist with the work of the Emissaries, the Commissions or the Archivist.

Implementation Suggestions

Appointing Emissaries: Poll all members on area(s) of interest.
Roles and Responsibilities of Emissaries:

- Continue work/interaction in area(s) of interest

  o Indicate, when appropriate, that you also represent the Council of Elders, and are looking for ways for the Council to assist in addressing issues of concern.

- Be *ATTENTIVE* to current and emerging issues in that area

- When issues arise, bring those issues to Council as a whole, for discussion on how to proceed, and whether further research/information gathering is needed.

- When appropriate, engage others within and beyond the Council to collect pertinent information regarding a particular issue. This may or may not require setting up a Commission for further study. If there are groups already working the issue in the community, the Emissaries job is to participate, where appropriate, in those community discussions to gather information to bring back to the Council. If no group is currently doing work around the issue, it may be necessary to set up a Commission for further information gathering.

Informational needs of the Council (this is what each Emissary is tasked to find out):

- What exactly is the issue? What are fundamental reasons the issue exists?

- How is the issue currently being addressed, if at all?

- What are possible solutions to the issue?

- Who needs to be involved with solutions?

- How can the Council assist?

Commissions:

Commissions are NOT standing committees. Commissions are only set up when this is the only way to gather the necessary information for Council decisions. The ultimate decision the Council will need to make (and thus, requiring information from the Commission), is if/how the Council can have a role in moving the community toward solutions of the issue. The Commission's role is to bring recommendations to the Council about how it might proceed on the issue being discussed. Commissions may be made up of individuals who are NOT Council of Elders members.

Associate Elders:

The Commissions represent an opportunity to invite those who might be considered "Associate Elders" to engage with the work of the Council. Thus, Associate Elders can/should only be invited in response to an actual need for their participation around an issue. If/once an issue is resolved, they may retain their Associate Elder status, if they've chosen to be identified as such. To do so, they may then be requested to pay dues (if the organization is set up for dues), although participation in the Council's monthly meetings should not be mandatory. A periodic meeting time may be established, aside from the regular monthly meeting of the Elders or at a designated Council meeting, to bring all Associate Elders together, to share information in their area(s) of expertise.

- Once an issue has been studied by the Commission, each Commission should delegate a Spokesperson to lead the discussion with the larger Council of Elders. Their report should include the elements listed above:

  o What exactly is the issue? What are fundamental reasons the issue exists?

  o How is the issue currently being addressed, if at all?

  o What are possible solutions to the issue?

  o Who needs to be involved with solutions?

  o How can the Council assist? (**Recommendation**)

The Commission should have all relevant information and data available to share with the larger Council. *As a note: the Spokesperson does not have to be a Council member, but may be an Associate Elder or anyone else <u>who has participated in the Commission's work</u>*.

Archivist:

An **archivist** is a professional who <u>assesses, collects, organizes, preserves, maintains control over, and provides access</u> to information determined to have long-term value. The information maintained by an archivist can be any form of media (ALL meeting minutes, photographs, video or sound recordings, letters, documents, electronic records, etc.).

Archivists are often educators as well; when appropriate, the Archivist has the responsibility of setting up exhibits, providing informational sessions, and sharing the history and work-to-date of the Council of Elders to the larger community.

Time should be set aside, periodically, for the Council Archivist to share a record of information currently contained in the Council Archives. This may be most appropriate as part of an orientation for new members *annually*.

Other Roles:

Depending on desires and work of the Council, there may be a need to fill other important roles, as well. For example, if the Council has financial matters that it undertakes (including dues, financial gifts, meeting expenses, etc.), there may be a need for a *Treasurer*. The role of *Recording/Corresponding Secretary* will probably also be needed. In addition, a standing committee may be required for ongoing recruitment of new members, and for planning and implementing regular Enstoolment ceremonies. Finally, because Elders may, in the course of their service, become infirm or have medical issues that disable them from full participation, there may be a standing committee that keeps them connected and works to keep them informed and engaged in the work of the Council, per their interests.

Secretary:

The role of Secretary is important for maintaining the continuity of records from each Council meeting. Ideally, the Secretary will record the primary information and decisions transacted at each meeting, as well as commitments for follow-up made during Council meetings, and planned agenda for upcoming meetings. These will be reviewed by the Presiding Elder between each meeting, and then distributed to each Elder along with the agenda for the upcoming meeting, PRIOR the next meeting. The Secretary and Presiding Elder should work together to make sure meeting information flows appropriately and in a timely manner. A *template has been provided in the Appendix to assist with this important function.*

Council of Elders

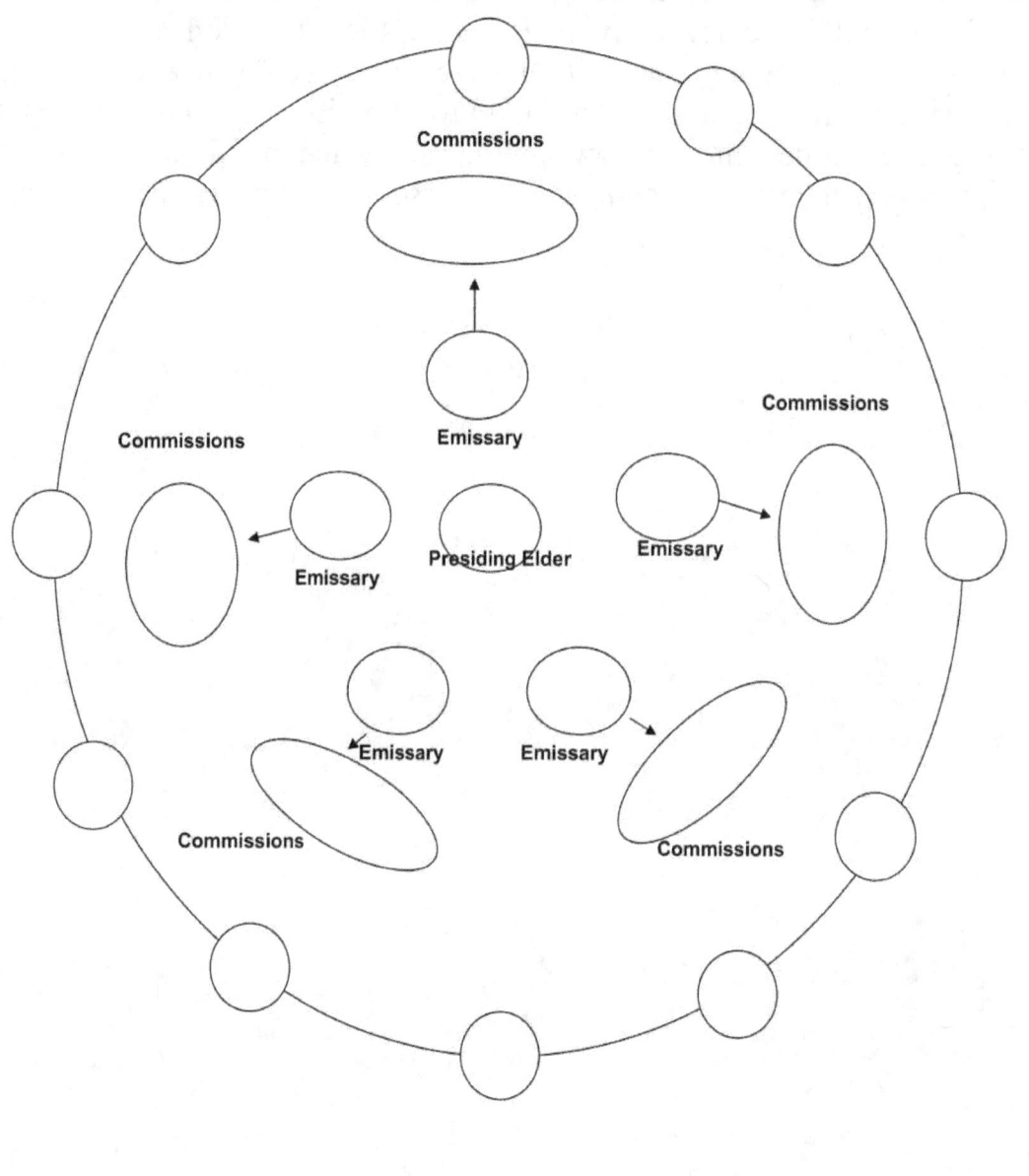

EPILOGUE:
Transforming our Communities

Although the concept of bodies such as the Council of Elders is not a new one, the re-instituting of such bodies, especially in African American and Native American communities across the United States, is a relatively new innovation. Not only does it appear necessary for community members to gain an understanding and appreciation of the potential inherent in such structures, but the Elders themselves have to re-conceptualize what it means to again be held in a position of guidance and accountability to the entire community. Especially in our modern social arrangement where senior citizens are often discarded or marginalized, to be reclaimed as a valuable resource and repository of the community's historical perspective and cultural values can be both heady and humbling. That the Elders on our local Council are taking very seriously the charge before them, and are proactively seeking ways to be meaningful change agents speaks well of their potential to actually be agents for change.

Because the Council in our community is a "new idea" and an innovation, there appears to be a need for the innovation to be diffused, even among them. Because of their internal diversity, coming to consensus regarding the nature of their responsibility as a body is a work-in-progress. However, as they become even more established, they will need to continue to utilize effective communication of community values, a coherent agenda, and their commitment to the community via methods that are persuasive, inclusive, multifaceted, and change-provoking.

Additionally, as other Councils of Elders are created in communities across the country and beyond, there is potential for regional and even a national Council of Elders. These Councils can be made up of local representatives who can share challenges, successes and skill-based learning among themselves to improve African American communities throughout the nation. At the time of this writing, there are efforts being made toward that end. There is even the potential that they will become an institutionalized regional and national voice for change that the carries the weight of the communities which they represent, and which can spread the values and principles that those communities hold as important and critical to our ongoing survival in this country, and beyond.

APPENDICES

Tools and Resources
To Start You on Your Journey

Steps to a Performing Community

Groups go through steps before they reach the performance level. These steps include gathering, chaos, unity, and performing. Below are the steps to a performing community, with the major tasks of each step, as applied generally to civic engagement and social capital building with identified community groups.

1. Gathering
"Why are we here and what do we have to contribute?"

The first step in a performing community is gathering. The primary tasks of the gathering step are about gaining a collective understanding of why those gathered are there and what they have to contribute. The act of gathering includes using strategic social capital building to identify and invite the right stakeholders to the table, setting the right meeting environment, gaining an understanding of the past to build upon, creating group norms, building collective servant leadership amongst group members, and identifying the individual strengths and assets of the stakeholders gathered.

2. Chaos
"What is our purpose?"

Before a group can effectively work together, it often experiences chaos. During the chaos step, a group experiences barriers to successful collaboration such as poor communication, lack of leadership, absence of vision and mission, and an inability to use conflict positively and constructively. Though individuals may understand the reason for the group and what it hopes to achieve, the means by which to reach those goals, as well as individual roles, may not be well-defined. Combined with limited resources, these barriers can make the chaos step frustrating. The task of bringing a group out of chaos is to define the group's purpose. The keys related to the task of moving a group through chaos and keeping members engaged in the change process include building trust, effective communication, defining roles, defining the vision and the "end-in-mind," and identifying community assets and resources.

3. Unity
"How will we do it?"

After a group overcomes the roadblocks to success that occur during chaos, it can then experience unity. Unity usually involves members working together to overcome the barriers they encountered during the chaos step. Specifically, the primary task of the unity step centers on defining how to accomplish the work and usually involves members using consensus decision processes to define common goals and objectives that capitalize on identified community and group member assets, as well as establishing tracking and feedback systems.

4. Performing
"Do it . . . What's next?"

After uniting as a group, a collaborative is then in a position to perform by doing the work and taking the next steps. Of particular importance is to maintain the group's momentum and make progress without overwhelming group members. Performing involves effective external communication, maintaining a vision focus, sharing leadership and work, reaching and following through on agreements by completing agreed upon tasks, and working actively to evaluate progress, celebrate wins, and course correct to make progress.

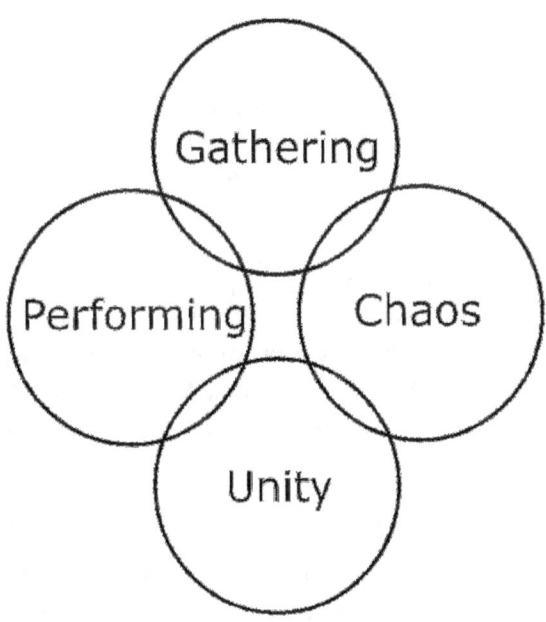

Pros and Cons of Non-Profit 501(c)3 Incorporation

By Neetal Parekh

Incorporating as a non-profit 501(c)3 organization provides an organization considerable tax benefits, but what are the drawbacks? Below are some pros and cons for filing for non-profit status.

Pros for incorporating as a non-profit 501(c)3 organization

- Pay no federal, state, or local taxes
- Qualify for special grants and government funding, even lower postage rates
- Encourage donation by providing donors with tax deduction
- Shield owners and directors from liability through status as a corporation
- Be eligible for discounted advertising rates, including possible free tv and radio public service announcements (PSA's)

Cons of incorporating as a non-profit 501(c)3 organization

- Lengthier, more-involved application and qualification process that requires payment of multiple fees and costs
- Must comply with numerous regulatory requirements, including submitting annual reports to federal and state agencies
- Can only pay managers reasonable salaries, can't divide profits equally.
- Can't pay Board of Directors
- On dissolution, must distribute assets to other non-profits

If you are debating between filing as a corporation or a non-profit 501(c)3 organization, take a moment to answer the questions below. They will help frame your organization's priorities and help you determine whether non-profit organization status or for-profit incorporation is the better fit.

Does your organization prefer flexibility over cost benefits?

Will your organization be more successful in securing funding by being able to offer a tax exemption for donations or will investors be more drawn by potential returns on investment?

Will your organization be able to attract high-quality leadership with any limits on compensation?

Despite the time and paperwork involved in filing as a 501(c)3 non-profit, will the status enable your organization to focus more time and resources on your mission or cause?

If you have additional questions or concerns about whether non-profit status is right for your organization, consult with an attorney who specializes in non-profit 501(c)3 incorporation.

Steps to Becoming an IRS Recognized Nonprofit Organization

1. Develop a mission statement and primary activities of the organization. Choose a name (with "Inc.", "Association", etc.).

2. Develop a group of incorporators who will help write bylaws and develop your IRS application. Once the bylaws are developed, these individuals may be interested in being elected as members of the Board of Directors.

3. Choose a primary contact person and principle office address.

4. Write the Articles of Incorporation (see sample) and submit AN ORIGINAL signed BY THE INCORPORATOR(S) witnessed by a notary public, with a check in the appropriate amount made out to the Secretary of State.

   You will receive a filed, stamped copy of your articles within 10 days.

5. Write the organization's bylaws (see sample). All board members should be familiar with the bylaws as they will guide the organization and are a contract with the state of Kansas regarding how you will run your organization. Once bylaws are completed, a Board and officers can be elected.

6. Go to the IRS website irs.gov and print the following forms. You may also call the IRS at 1-800-829-3676 for the following forms to become a nonprofit organization:
   - SS-4
   - 1023
   - 2848

7. Fill out and sign the SS-4 form in order to receive your Federal Employee Identification Number (FEIN) and fax to Entity Control to 215-516-3990 (or you may do this by phone at 1-800-829-4933). You will need this number on other IRS forms you will be submitting.

8. Fill out the above IRS forms (SS-4, 1023, and 2848) referring to publication 556 and instructions for form 1023. It is important to have an experienced attorney (with nonprofits) review your bylaws and IRS application in advance of submittal to IRS. It is recommended that this attorney be given power of attorney status using the IRS 2848 form. This will allow him or her to check on the status of the application and answer any questions IRS representatives may have. Send ALL the IRS forms with signatures, signed bylaws, and a copy of the filed, stamped articles of incorporation along with a copy of the initial articles, with a check for the appropriate amount made out to the United States Treasury.

Guiding Principles and Small Group Exercise

step #1

Each person in the group should take a few minutes to answer the following questions from their personal perspective:

1) What are the principles and policies that should guide how we work include? _____

_____

_____

_____

_____

_____

_____

2) What are the values that we believe in and should express through our work?_____

_____

_____

_____

_____

_____

_____

Step #2

After writing individual answers, discuss in your small group or as a whole, if the group is small enough (less than 15) . Have someone record the answers on a flip chart.

- Take about 10-15 minutes to do Step #2 and don't forget to designate a recorder and a reporter!

Step #3

If done in small groups, have a large group call out. Each small group calls out in value added manner, meaning, if a response is already recorded, do not re-record. Record on a flip chart.

Step #4

If a larger group, garner a commitment from small sub-group (no more than 2-4 people) to develop draft guiding principles from the information generated for review at a later time by the larger group.

Guiding Principles for Working Together

Clarify your organization's belief systems: • What are some of the values, beliefs, and/or guiding principles that should guide our work together?	Practical impact: • What are the behaviors we commit to doing in this process to support these values?
• As a Core Team	•
• As we Coordinate with Other Interested Groups	•
• With The Community, as a whole	•
With Business Groups and Organizations •	•

*** Be sure to identify all possible stakeholders to identify principles for quality work with them.

Vision/Brainstorming Tools

The framing question

Often an issue can be presented or visioning can be introduced by asking the group a framing question. One powerful and flexible question is "What would it look like if we got it right?" "It" can be an issue, a community, a process or anything else the group cares about.

After presenting the issue for discussion (often in the form of a question), write it on a flipchart and keep it in front of the group.

Open brainstorming

Establish the following ground rules for brainstorming:

- Do not discuss ideas

- Do not judge ideas

- Repeating ideas is fine

- Piggybacking ideas is fine

- Wait for silences to end – the greatest creativity may follow

- The more ideas the better

Quickly record ideas so everyone can read them as they are shared. Do not filter the ideas; just record them as they are presented. Continue listing ideas until all ideas are exhausted. Briefly discuss, clarify, and consolidate the listed ideas.

Value-added brainstorming (also called round robin brainstorming)

Define the issue and write it on a flipchart (see above). Ask participants to write down three ideas on the brainstorming topic. Provide index cards and pens. Participants work alone quietly. After a few minutes, ask participants to independently prioritize their ideas using (A, B, and C).

Start a Value Added Call Out. The first participant calls out his/her top priority idea. The second calls out his/her top idea unless it is the same as the first idea that was shared. In that case, the second participant calls out his/her second priority idea. This continues until all ideas are exhausted and recorded. As an option, you can ask the group to indicate if they had also listed an idea and keep a tally.

Discuss and consolidate ideas.

Affinity brainstorming (also called "theming")

Define the issue and write it on a flipchart (see above). Ask participants to write down all their ideas on 3x5 sticky notes (i.e., Post-it notes) – only one idea per note. Conduct a Call and Sort activity. Ask a participant to read one of his/her notes and place it on a flipchart. Ask if anyone has written down a similar idea and read each note as it is placed on the flipchart. Ask the group to name the natural relationship between the ideas and record it on the flipchart with the sticky notes. These identified natural relationships can be referred to as themes. Continue to call and sort ideas until all sticky notes are posted on flipcharts. Allow sticky notes to be moved as the group refines the natural relationships between their ideas.

Preceding brainstorming tools are from Ray, R.G. (1999). The Facilitative Leader: Behaviors that Enable Success.

Multiple lens

Define the issue and write it on a flipchart (see above). Using index cards or Post-Its, assign individuals or small groups each the role of a citizen group that has a stake in the issue. These roles might reflect age, gender, ethnicity, profession, place of residence, political party or side of a community issue. The facilitator should explain that while we can't know what another person wants, needs or thinks, we can stretch our thinking and use what we do know to consider another point of view.

Each individual or small group considers what solutions would be "just right" for the role it is representing. Record these solutions and call them out to the larger group. Debrief with questions such as, "What assumptions that we previously made are challenged by these ideas?" and "What themes recur in several groups?"

Because multiple lens can lead to charged but powerful conversations, especially when used to consider difficult issues, it should be selected and facilitated with care. At the same time, it can lead to fun and creative conversations when used to help plan a project, such as a community center or festival. It is also useful as a "check-back" after a group has initially made a decision to help ensure that all perspectives are considered.

Draw your vision

The willingness and ability to envision a preferred future is a creative process. Naturally, some people will express their visions creatively as well. An individual or group vision may take the form of a poem, a dance, a song – or a drawing.

One process for drawing a vision follows a time of individual reflection, such as a guided imagery "dream" of an organization's future. After dreaming and reflecting on their own, the participants take a few minutes to share the experience with one other person. Next, small groups form and talk about what they envisioned. Together, the small group members draw one picture incorporating the core themes from their individual visions. These pictures are presented and explained to the full group.

The facilitator(s) helps the group to identify and build consensus around common themes. Before the group moves on to setting goals and taking action, a volunteer from each of the small groups is identified. These volunteer "Vision Painters" draw the common visions of the whole group. Alternatively, everyone can be involved in creating a collage of the group's common vision rather than a common portrait.

Draw Your Vision tool from Trustee Leadership Development (1997). <u>Preparing Leaders and Nurturing Trustees: Educator's Manual</u>.

Mission Statements

The purpose of an agency's mission statement is to relate:

- WHAT is going to be done

- WHY it is done

- WHO is going to be served

Mission statement example

"The African American Council of Elders will support family strengthening in Kansas communities, in order to increase family efficacy that will support school achievement and educational completion for all African American youth in Kansas."

Mission statements:

- Relate the agency's special task or purpose

- Should be no more than a paragraph—the shorter the better

- Are a useful tool to measure potential new direction against—"Is this in keeping with our mission?"

- Show that different agencies may have the same/similar mission statements

Mission statement: small group exercise

Step #1

Each person takes a few minutes to individually answer the following questions from their personal perspective:

1) The Council of Elders will do (action)_____

_____

_____

_____

2) For whom (who do we serve?)_____

_____

_____

_____

3) So that (result of our action)_____

_____

_____

_____

Step #2

After writing individual answers, discuss in your small group. Have someone record the answers on a flip chart.

- Please take about 10-15 minutes to do Step #2 and don't forget to designate a recorder and a reporter!

Step #3

Large group call out. Each small group calls out in value added manner (don't repeat same information other small group has already called out). Record on a flip chart.

Step #4

Commitment from small sub-group (no more than 2-4 people) to develop a draft mission statement from the information generated for review at a later time by the larger group.

Identifying Objectives: Small Group Exercise

Strategy_____

_____

_____

Step #1

Take a few moments to think about the NEXT YEAR and what you feel needs to be accomplished for THIS STRATEGY. Small groups can consider each strategy or different small groups can work on a strategy each. Letting group members self select to the strategy of greatest interest often works well.

Step #2

Then AS A GROUP talk about the following question and come up with 2 or 3 "do-able" objectives for this strategy.

1) We will _____(action),

2) With the target of _____ (how much/many)

3) by _____ (date).

Step #3

Have someone record the objectives on a flip chart so that they can be "called-out" to the large group. Please take about 15-20 minutes to do Steps #1-3 and don't forget to designate a recorder and a reporter!

Step #4

Large group call out. Each small group calls out in value added manner for each strategy. Record on a flip chart.

Step #5

Commitment from small sub-group (no more than 2-4 people) to develop draft objectives from the information generated for review at a later time by the larger Council. It is important to review these draft statements with those actually responsible for meeting the objectives (e.g., Council members, volunteer) and stakeholders who are actually targeted by the objectives.

Identifying Strategies: Small group Exercise

Step #1

As a group, take a few minutes to reflect on the Council's mission, goals and/or guiding principles (if they've been developed as part of a strategic planning process) and identify and list the driving forces (i.e., strengths that will help support the mission, goals and/or guiding principles) and restraining forces (i.e., barriers that might inhibit mission, goals and/or guiding principles success) using the following format:

Driving forces	Restraining forces

Strategies:

Don't forget to designate a group recorder, facilitator and reporter!

Step #2

As a group, use the identified driving and restraining forces to brainstorm strategies that support the mission, goals and/or guiding principles using the strategy guidelines (see p. 11). List the strategies on the table shown in Step #1 above.

Step #3

Large group call out. Each small group calls out in value added manner. Record on a flip chart.

Step #4

As a large group theme out the primary, global strategies so that consensus is gained on the HOW (e.g., public awareness, advocacy, research) then gain a commitment from small sub-group (no more than 2-4 people) to develop a draft strategy statements from the information generated for review at a later time by the larger Council.

Action steps

An organization's action steps will relate:

- WHAT is the specific action step
- WHEN it will be completed
- WHO is responsible

Examples of Actions Steps

WHEN	WHAT	WHO
2/23	First meeting of planning team	Shakil
3/1	Begin community input process	Planning Team
04/03	Review data	Research Team
05/02	Develop nomination processes	Sheila and Jon
06/03	Solicit Nominations	Planning Team

Action steps:

- Action-oriented, not procedural
- More than one action step may be needed for each strategy
- Should consider external/internal constraints
- Compared with other options, chosen based on: potential benefit, and cost/consequences

Identifying action steps small group exercise

Objective_____

_____

_____

step #1

Take a few moments to think about the NEXT SIX MONTHS and what you believe needs to be accomplished for this OBJECTIVE.

step #2

Then AS A GROUP use the following exercise to come up with 3 or 4 action steps in this objective.

When	What	Who	Who Else

step #3

Have someone record the action steps on a flip chart so that they can be "called-out" to the large group.

Please take about 15-20 minutes to do Steps #1-3 and don't forget to designate a recorder and a reporter!

step #4

Large group call out. Each small group calls out action steps in a value added manner for each objective. Record on a flip chart.

step #5

Commitment typically from same small sub-group who are developing objectives to develop draft action steps from the information generated for review at a later time by the larger group. It is important to review these draft statements with those actually responsible for the action steps (e.g., staff, volunteer). Small sub-groups typically generated more concrete and accurate action steps than do large, whole group processes.

Asset Mapping Explanation

Purpose

At times, it may be useful for you or a small group to begin identifying assets and strengths within a community. The following asset inventory provides a useful set of questions to address when identifying the assets within a given group, organization, or community. The asset inventory provides a starting point for greater understanding and intentional identification of those assets and strengths that may normally be overlooked or taken for granted. The inventory can be completed individually or in a small group setting. Additional steps would need to be taken to mobilize those assets and strengths once they are identified.

Benefits

The asset inventory is a quick and easy-to-use set of questions that can provide a lot of information in a short period of time. It can be used individually or in a small group setting to identify those individuals, groups, and organizations that can help in addressing a particular problem or issue facing the community.

Instructions

Provide an opportunity for everyone to reflect on the following list of questions so they can identify the usual and not-so-usual assets and strengths within their community.

Asset Inventory Example

Problem, Issue, or Concern Being Addressed:

Increase high school completion rate for USD 332, Gypsum County

Geographic Area of the Community:

Greater Wasaum City

Assets (Resources) Needed:

Engagement of: faith communities, healthcare professionals, schools, mass media, social services, youth professionals and volunteers, youth groups; money; training for individual and group counseling; places to meet in groups and one-on-one; educational materials; time of people; mentors for children and youth.

Individuals (with Note about Talents and Skills):

- Clarise Dunnagin – School board member

- Jamil Asaad – volunteer who works with disadvantaged households

- Sheila Turner – Youth counselor and program coordinator for community mentoring program

- Damon Dessarte– former County Commissioner, with multiple contacts and people resources at all levels

Citizen Associations in the Community:

- Parent/Teacher Resource Councils

- Neighborhood Associations that cover areas where our students live/attend school

- Gypsum County Human Services Coalition

- Black Ministerial Alliance

- Wasaum City United Way

- Faith communities

Institutions in the Community:

- Kansas Department of Social and Rehabilitation Services

- Wasaum University Outreach and Extension

- Kansas Department of Elementary and Secondary Education

- Boys and Girls Club of Central Kansas

- Kansas Department of Mental Health

- Kansas Department of Health

- University of Kansas hospitals and clinics

- Wasaum Safety Net Clinics Association

- Area schools

- Community Policing Department

Asset Inventory Worksheet

Problem, Issue, or Concern Being Addressed:

Geographic Area of the Community:

Assets (Resources) Needed:

Individuals (with Note about Talents and Skills):

Citizen Associations in the Community:

Institutions in the Community:

Nomination to
The African American Council of Elders Pt. 1

Nominee Name _____ Age _____ Birth Date _____

Address of Nominee _____ Phone No. _____

E-mail Address: _____ M/F _____

Currently employed? Yes ____ No ____if Yes, where: _____

What areas(s) or field(s) of interest has this individual worked/served in while living in [City]? (Please limit to a maximum of three [3].)

Law	Government	Religion
Social/Human Services	Education	Business
Finance	Media	Family Strengthening
Other (Please Specify) _____		

Please check here to indicate if this person is being nominated for Associate Elder or other status.

Name of Nominating Person (if other than Nominee) _____

Relationship to Nominee _____ Phone No. _____

• •

African American Elders Councils exist in many selected cities and communities across the United States. Elders are a necessary and integral part of any functioning African and African American community.

On an attached sheet, please state clearly and concisely the reasons you feel this individual would be willing, able and committed to being part of the African American Council of Elders. In your response, please address the following qualifications and criteria: *Maturity, Wisdom and Spirituality; Respect, Knowledge of Youth and Commitment to Youth; Commitment to the African American community; and Community Affiliations (i.e. social, civic or religious organizations).* The more information provided, the better we will be able to assess the candidate's suitability for the Council. Please be sure to include Nominee's name on the attached sheet.

The reverse side of this form is the Nominee's application for membership. ***THIS MUST BE COMPLETED BY THE NOMINEE***, as an indication that they have been provided information about the Council of Elders and that they are interested in serving the community in this capacity.

The African American Council of Elders
Membership Application – Pt. 2

Nominee Name _____

Please review information on the reverse side of this form to insure its accuracy. Is the information accurate? If not, please make the appropriate changes.

Have you read the information provided on the African American Council of Elders?
Yes/No _____

Are you interested in serving our community in this capacity? Yes/No _____

If yes, what do you feel you can bring to the work of the Council of Elders and why? (Please feel free to attach an addition sheet, if more space needed.)

I am willing to use my talents and skills to serve the community through the work of the Council in the areas indicated below:

Organizing (events/activities

Programs

Neighborhood Outreach/Forums

Political outreach (forums/voter registration)

Clerical (filing/writing/typing)

Teaching (tutoring/mentoring/curriculum development/workshops)

Other _____

Finance (grant/budget/fund raising)

Artistic (music/crafts/performing)

Can/Will you make yourself available for a ½ day orientation? Yes/No _____

Please indicate if you have any accessibility needs: _____

_____

Emergency Contact Information (Name/Phone Number): _____

Doctor/Hospital _____ **Other:** _____

_____   _____
Nominee Signature   Date

_____   _____

Sample Agenda for TCOE Pre-Enstoolment Orientation

TIME	ACTIVITY	*OBJECTIVES:*	WHO?
Seating	Pass out Tootsie Roll Pops and Elders arrive, dividing them evenly between the three colors. Ask them to please sit at the tables designated for the color of their sucker. Hand out Talent and Interest Inventories (including those already turned in), and Who's On the Council questionnaire.	*To have Elders seated in random groupings in preparation for exercises and processes..*	Scribes or Facilitators
12:00 – 1:00	Opening Libations/Prayer - Lunch		
1:00 – 1:20	Introduction/Ice Breaker Housekeeping	*An icebreaker that can be done as people drift in…to bring everyone "into the circle."*	Scribes or Facilitators
1:20 – 1:40	"Why A Council of Elders?"	*Background and History of TCOE* *Q & A re: background*	Scribes or Facilitators
1:40 – 1:50	Vision/Mission Overview (By-laws)	*To review TCOE Vision/Mission Statement and clarify work of TCOE*	Scribes or Facilitators Knox
1:50 – 2:50	On a Mission: Beginning the Work (Brainstorm Activity)	*To determine what concrete activities TCOE might involve itself in to further and fulfill its vision and mission.*	Scribes or Facilitators
2:50 – 3:00	Break		

TIME	ACTIVITY	OBJECTIVES:	WHO?
3:00 – 3:20	Personal Mission/Interest Inventory - In small groups, have participants split into groups of no more than four, select a recorder and reporter and talk about their Talent/Interest Inventory and how those fit into the vision/mission of the organization, and with the activities the Council has set for itself over the next year.	*(In small groups) To assist participants to determine how their own personal mission and interests fit in with the overall mission of the Council.*	Scribes or Facilitators
3:20 – 3:45	Commitment and Continuance - Have group reporters report on their groups' commitments.	*To allow Council members to make a public commitment of how they would like to be involved with TCOE – based on ideas for continuance*	Scribes or Facilitators
3:45 – 4:00	Calling Tree Explanation and Demonstration – *The Importance of Being in Touch*	*To demonstrate a method for periodic and ongoing communication among TCOE members*	Scribes or Facilitators
4:00 – 5:00	Enstooling Particulars – Date, Time, Dress, ceremony, etc. (Pass out shawls and switches to enstooled Elders.)	*To provide information on the upcoming Enstooling activities, and to answer any questions.*	Scribes or Facilitators

WHO'S ON THE COUNCIL? EXERCISE

Read the following questions. In small groups (not more than five), take turns asking each other any questions you wish to answer. You may answer with the first response that comes to mind. There are no right answers, only how you perceive things. You do not have to answer the question if you don't want to, but you may not ask a question that you don't want to answer.

1. What is the most important concern in your life right now?

2. Who is the most important person in your life right now?

3. If you could change anything about our community, what would you change?

4. What message do you have for our youth?

5. What are your major goals right now? Do you have the resources to reach them?

6. What are your goals for this organization?

*Decide on a spokesperson for your group to discuss your answers.

Sample
Rites of Passage – Enstooling Ceremony

Date_____ Time: _____

(A scribe should ensure that seating is set up with chairs facing the assemboy for the Enstoolees to sit. Each enstoolee must have an Elders assigned to her/him prior to the ceremony. All participants should be lined up at least 30 minutes prior to the ceremony. The plant and water should be placed where the Enstoolees, Presiding Elder, and the Officiating Officer (Elder) will stand. The Sponsors (Elders) should carry the Kente for their assigned Enstoolees.

Introductory Rites	
Vice Presiding Elder	Friends, Family, Elders and Enstoolees may the God of all peace and understanding be with you.
All Elders	And also with you
Statement of Purpose	
Vice Presiding Elder	My brothers and sisters in Faith, we are gathered here today for a special and unique occasion, the Enstooling of candidates to membership in the African American Council of Elders ~ Wichita/Sedgwick County, Kansas

The African American Council of Elders has a disntinctive role and responsibility in the African American community, the City of Wichita, and the Nation as a whole. The Council is a circle of women and men – African American – or of African descent, whose mission and purpose are rooted in the seven principles of Kwanzaa, to advance the collective well being of African Americans, others of African descent, and ultimately all citizens of the City, State, Nation and World. The Council of Elders serves as a spiritual and ethical conduit for the Black community by building on the historical legacy of its African ancestry.

In carrying out its role, the Council of Elders pursues the following goals:

To serve as a role model to parents and youth;
To provide wisdom and direction in the struggle for freedom, justice and equity;
To preserve the history, traditions, and contributions of people of African descent;
To instruct, support, counsel and guide parents and youth; and
To address issues concerning the family, the village and the broader community.

Today, (number) candidates, called Enstoolees, are presenting themselves before the Council of Elders and the Community. As persons of great honor, integrity, and respect among their families, their peers, and the community, they eagerly seek entry into this Council of Elders. Therefore, as the voice of the Council of Elders, I welcome everyone here to witness their commitment to our mission. And now I ask that our Presiding Elder (name) and our |

	Officiating Elder (name) to come forward for the Rites of Passage – the Enstooling of our new members.
Calling Forth the Enstoolees	
Presiding Elder	Officiating Elder (name), these Enstoolees, who I present to you, have completed their final period of preparation for the Rites of Passage into the Council of Elders. They have found strength in God's grace and support in our community. They have demonstrated through their personal actions of love, devotion, and dedication toward our community and toward one another. Now, they ask that they be recognized for the progress they have made in their spiritual formation, and that they receive the assurance of our blessings and prayers as they go forth to the Rites of Passage, as Enstoolees in the celebration today. I present to you the Officiating Officer of this ceremony, Elder (name).
Officiating Elder	Those who have been called to this celebration of the Rites of Passage for the Council of Elders, please come forward accompanied by your Sponsor.
Presiding Elder	Enstoolee (name), please come forward. *(Each Enstoolee is individually called forward by name. The sponsoring Elder of the Council accompanies each Enstoolee with the Kente on her/his arm. The Enstoolees and the Sponsor will stand behind their designated chairs facing the assembly.)* Enstoolees and Sponsors please be seated as we listen to the wisdom of the Officiating Elder (name). (All on stage be seated.)
Officiating Elder	Enstoolees, you have been preparing for your Rites of Passage into the Council of Elders. According to the testimony of witnesses in the Community, you have been found ready, willing and able to commit Yourself to your own ongoing spiritual and emotional growth, and to continuing service toward your fellow Elders, toward this community, and toward your God. God will be the final evaluator of your service, and your readiness and willingness to reach out to the least of your brothers and sisters in order to improve their position in the world. If this is your will, then this community is asking you to demonstrate your commitment and readiness by responding affirmatively to the following questions by stating: "I am ready, willing and able to make this commitment." Are you ready, willing and able to support the core values of the Council of Elders, based on the seven principles of Kwanzaa: Unity in the family and community; self-determination; collective work and responsibility; cooperative economics; purpose; creativity; and faith?
Enstoolees	I am ready, willing and able to make this commitment.
Officiating Elder	Are you ready, willing and able to preserve and transmit to our youth and the community, our history, traditions, contributions and gifts as people of African descent?

Enstoolees	I am ready, willing and able to make this commitment.
Officiating Elder	Are you reading, willing and able to serve as a role model to our youth in the African American and other communities; and to instruct, support and guide them in responsible leadership?
Enstoolees	I am ready, willing and able to make this commitment.
Officiating Elder	Are you ready, willing and able to provide to our youth and our people, wisdom and direction in their struggle for freedom, justice, equity and truth?
Enstoolees	I am ready, willing and able to make this commitment.
Officating Elder	Are you ready, willing and able to continue your own spiritual journey so that you may grow in strength, perseverance, wisdom, compassion and love – necessary ingredients in the struggle for freedom and justice?
Enstoolees	I am ready, willing and able to make this commitment.
Officiating Elder	Are you ready, willing and able to abide by and to support enthusiastically the vision, the mission, and the purpose of the Council of Elders as outlined and listed our Constitution and Bylaws, along with other provisions placed before you in this Rite of Passage? If so, then, please state: "I am ready, willing and able to make this commitment with the help of Almighty God."
Enstoolee	I am ready, willing and able to make this commitment with the help of Almighty God.
(At this time all on stage will stand. The Sponsoring Elders will stand beside the Enstoolees with the Kente cloth visible to the Assembly. Water and a live plant [representing the earth] should be on stage.)	
Officiating Elder	Enstoolees, please receive the Kente Cloth as a sign of your authority, respect, integrity, and wisdom within our Community.
(Sponsoring Elders face the Enstoolees and places the Kente Cloth over the shoulders of the newly installed Elders.)	
Officiating Elder	Enstoolees, water in our faith traditions represents repentance, cleanliness, the giving of life, and initiation into the faith community. Today, you are being initiated, and as a sign of your entry into our community – The African American Council of Elders – each individual please take the cup and pour it into the earth. When you finish pouring your portion, please say "Ashe" which means "so be it."
(The first sponsor takes the plant and moves from one Enstoolee to another as the water is poured. Each Enstoolee is to pour a few drops of water into the earth and pass the picture to the next Enstoolee, from right to left.)	
Enstoolees:	Ashe
Officiating Elder	Enstoolees, the community gladly accepts you as new Elders. May God bring to completion the good work that God has started in you.
Blessing the Elders	
Officiating Elder	Let us now in this assembly extend our hands of blessing over our new Elders, that we may be renewed in the heart, mind and spirit by their acceptance of their role in the community and by their willingness to continue to do God's work in spite of the trials facing them. (With hands extended, the final Prayer and Blessings are said.) God of love and power, it is your will to establish everything according to your order, and to draw us into your all-embracing love and concern for your people. Guide these newly installed Elders in the days and weeks ahead,

	strengthen them in their duties and responsibilities as they face what is before them, build them into your heavenly and eternal kingdom, and seal them with promise. We ask this prayer and all good things in You, with You and through YOU. Let us all say "Amen and Ashe."
Procession of New Elders	
Officiating Elder	All assembled here and in the community of Wichita, Kansas, I present to you the newly installed Elders of the African American Council of Elders ~ Wichita/Sedgwick County.

OATH TO THE ANCESTORS AND LIBATION STATEMENT

OATH TO OUR ANCESTORS
By Pastor Ray Hagins, Chief Elder & Spiritual Leader
The Afrikan Village and Cultural Center
 St. Louis, Missouri
www.wblr.com

O Ancestors! Blacker than a thousand midnights.
Afrikan Ancestors! It is to YOU that we, your children, give respect and honor.

O Ancestors! We call upon YOU and welcome you in this place.
Afrikan Ancestors! Let your presence fill this place.

O Ancestors! Who have been purposely excluded from the history books, so that the world would not know of your greatness.

Our Afrikan Ancestors! Who gave civilization to the world.
Our Afrikan Ancestors! Who gave the arts to the world.
Our Afrikan Ancestors! Who gave music to the world!
Our Afrikan Ancestors! Who gave the sciences to the world.
Our Afrikan Ancestors! Who gave mathematics to the world!
Our Afrikan Ancestors! Who gave medicine to the world!
Our Afrikan Ancestors! Who gave literature to the world!
Our Afrikan Ancestors! Who gave philosophy to the world!
Our Afrikan Ancestors! Who gave God consciousness to the world!

O Ancestors! We thank you for devoting your life to make a future for us, your children, grand children, and great grandchildren.

Now, stand with us; strengthen us; guide us; teach us, and protect us from the snare of our enemies!

Rise up, O Afrikan Ancestors, and let our enemies be scattered! And give us the wisdom and the boldness to deal with our oppressors and those who would hinder the liberation and empowerment of our people.

Rise up, O Afrikan Ancestors, and live in us.

We will not fail to honor you;
We will not fail to respect you;
We will not fail to hear you;
And we will NOT betray you!

Ase!

LIBATION STATEMENT

For The Motherland cradle of civilization.

For the ancestors and their indomitable spirit

For the elders from whom we can learn much.

For our youth who represent the promise for tomorrow.

For our people the original people.

For our struggle and in remembrance of those who have struggled on our behalf.

For Umoja the principle of unity which should guide us in all that we do.

For the creator who provides all things great and small.

TIMELINE PROCESS

<u>Purpose/objectives</u>

This is a simple process that can be useful when initially gathered newly seated elders to encourage a sense of shared experiences and community knowledge.

It can also be used as a tool to gather information from medium to large community group gatherings to discern salient issues that the community would like to see addressed.

One of the greatest benefits of the timeline process is the power it has to help people gain a better awareness and appreciation for each other's experiences, strengths, and perspectives. It is also a great tool for helping people identify what they have in common through the stories that are told.

<u>Benefits</u>

- Create a sense of community within a group by providing a shared experience and shared identity based on the past.

- Provide insight into complex issues.

- Help people work through difficult history and lead a group toward healing.

- Bridge the past with the present and the future.

- Help participants appreciate the "lens" through which other people in the group view things.

- Facilitate documentation of lost stories.

- Reveal issues that need work and lead to intentional action to resolve those issues.

- Lift up the values by which the group functions.

<u>Background</u>

As the Council of Elders begins its work together, it will be important that their individual histories and shared histories can ultimately evolve into a shared history of the community and Council. Routine decisions and actions can then be made based on this shared history and the vision that is derived from it. Conducting a timeline process can be an incredible way to reconnect with the past to understand the present and plan for the future.

You do not have to be a history expert to facilitate a timeline process. In fact, knowing too much about a group's history can actually hinder a good facilitation if you do not resist interjecting your knowledge. For the group to own their history, they need to create it themselves.

<u>Materials Needed</u>

- 1 black marker for every 2 or 3 people (to use for signing-in on the timeline).

- 2 sets of broad point markers in bright colors (for drawing and for capturing ah-has during the timeline).

- 3 to 4 feet wide newsprint long enough to cover at least 12 to 15 feet of wall space. More people and a longer time frame will require more newsprint.

- Pre-made flipchart—"Key Early Markers" (if applicable—see facilitation outline below).

- Masking tape measuring 1 to 2 inches in width or self-sticking flipchart paper.

- Flipchart paper (to record ah-has and debriefing notes).

- Optional—Quotations for posting near the timeline wall or around the room that speak to the relevance of history and the value of reflection. Possible quotes include:

  "Without roots, plants perish. Without history, the present makes no sense. Without a historical base, a vision is rootless and doomed."—Lee Bolman and Terrence Deal
  "Sometimes a person has to go back—really back—to have a sense, an understanding of all that's gone to make them—before they can go forward."— Paula Marshall
  "He who learns, teaches." ~ African Proverb
  "For tomorrow belongs to the people who prepare for it today." ~ African Proverb
  "It takes a village to raise a child." ~ African Proverb
  "Until lions have their historians, tales of the hunt shall always glorify the hunter" ~ African Proverb
  "If you want to know the end, look at the beginning" ~ African Proverb
  "A wise man never knows all, only fools know everything." ~ African Proverb
  "The young can't teach traditions to the old." ~ African Proverb
  "When you are at home, your troubles can never defeat you." ~ African Proverb
  "People know each other better on a journey." ~ African Proverb
  "That which is good is never finished." ~ African Proverb

<u>Preparing for the timeline</u>

Facilitation Team—To successfully facilitate a timeline process, two people are necessary. One important purpose of the timeline process is to help groups work together more effectively. Good facilitators model what they teach, including working with a partner. In addition to modeling how to work together, two people are needed so one can record information on the timeline while the other facilitates the conversation. It is nearly impossible for one person to effectively fulfill both roles.

Room Arrangement—Ideally, the room will be large enough to accommodate a seating area separate from the rest of the day's activities with a large blank wall on which to post the timeline paper. Find a long wall with good lighting where you can gather participants in a semi-circle. For groups of 15 or more you will need to have 2 to 3 rows with all seats facing the timeline wall.

Preliminary Set-Up

- Roll out a piece of newsprint 12 to 15 feet long and then double back over it. Tape the two layers together (you need two layers to avoid markers soaking though to the wall). With your co-facilitator, tape the paper to the wall high enough that everyone will be able to see it (but not so high that you can't draw/write on it), and use ample tape so it doesn't fall down.

- Draw a horizontal line the length of the paper, dividing the paper into two approximately equal sections (top and bottom).

- Using vertical lines, mark time segments that make sense for the group (e.g., decades), depending on the possible earliest birth year of those in the group.

- Place a set of markers in an easy-to-access location. You will use these to capture people's stories on the timeline.

- On a separate piece of flipchart paper, make an instruction sheet. Instructions might include:

1. Write your name on the timeline noting when you first entered this community (possibly at birth).
2. Draw an image symbolizing a pivotal event in the history of your life in this community.

- Place several markers of one color near the timeline for participants to use for signing-in. Offer only one color so you can distinguish your writing from the sign-in information.

- Select and post quotes relevant to the issue of reflection and history (see above quotes).

- Set up a separate flipchart pad to use in recording "ah-has" at the end of the timeline.

- Arrange chairs in front of the timeline in a semi-circle, allowing only enough room for the two facilitators to work along the timeline. Place all chairs facing the wall. If necessary, make 2 to 3 rows of chairs to accommodate all participants.

Frequently asked questions

Is there ever a time when it is not appropriate to use the timeline process?

Even though this exercise helps to understand the past, it is not a history lesson. The content of the timeline depends on the knowledge and experiences of those present. Very often, the group does not collectively possess everything there is to know about history, particularly of the community, state, country, and world. Thus, it would be a mistake to expect the group to adequately serve in this purpose. It is more important for the timeline to function as a tool to facilitate shared understanding than it is for the timeline to be factually accurate. Other means may be needed to address questions regarding the facts of history. If it is critical to the outcome of the timeline process for the facts to be accurate, we would encourage you to do some research in advance and offer that to the group as part of the information recorded on the timeline prior to the meeting. History should never be used to justify the status quo or behaviors of the past, only to understand what happened.

How long will the timeline take?

Our experience doing timelines with groups suggests that, depending on the number of people involved and the issues that need to be drawn out, the timeline process can take an average of 1.5 hours (for less than 10 people) to 3 hours (for 30 or more people).

Could we save time by skipping the debriefing at the end?

The timeline discussion that precedes the debriefing is really the "means to the end" of what comes out of the debriefing. Skipping the debriefing would be like driving to the grocery store and turning around to go home without stopping to buy your groceries. Though the timeline process does require an investment of time, we have never found it to be a waste of time as a first step in helping groups think about their future.

Is it possible to do the timeline with a different seating arrangement?

If space makes the semi-circle arrangement around the timeline wall impossible, you can use other seating arrangements; however there are distinct advantages to the semi-circle arrangement. When the group sits close together facing the wall, the arrangement creates a sense of closeness and promotes honest, but informal conversation and storytelling (kind of like sitting around a fireplace). This seating arrangement also makes it easier for individuals in groups who do not know each other very well or are dealing with conflict to talk more openly because they are talking to the wall and the facilitators rather than directly to each other.

About the facilitator notes

The facilitator notes for the timeline process appear in worksheet format. There is space for you to indicate who is responsible for a portion of the presentation and at what time each activity will occur. In addition, the facilitator notes include an outline and a detailed script. This helpful reference key reminds you when to change slides, when there is a group activity or discussion, when to hand out worksheets, when to emphasize important points and opportunities for practical application, and even when to suggest supplemental reading.

Outline		
Who	**Time**	**Description**

		Outline:
		
		 I. Introduction
		 II. Gathering Activity
		 III. Explanation of the Timeline Process
		      A. Purpose
		      B. Benefits
		      C. Group Instructions
		 IV. Framing/Background
		 V. Facilitated Discussion
		 VI. Debrief the Discussion
		 VII. Wrap-Up/Transition

Some of the material included in this document was adapted from Mary Jo Clark and Pat Heiny's, *Timeline: A Complete Guide to Facilitation.* Much thanks goes to them for their authentic modeling as servant leaders who frequently share in deed, formal training, and materials their wisdom and know-how regarding community leadership and facilitation.

Timeline Facilitators' Discussion Guide
Gathering Activity: As with any other facilitation process, the timeline process should be conducted after you conduct appropriate framing and gathering activities.
Explanation of the Process: Let's begin answering who we are/want to be as an Council by assembling at the wall for what's called a timeline process.
- Purpose – There are a lot of different timeline processes and approaches – all are designed to help groups understand the importance and impact of historical events in shaping the current status of an organization/group.

- Benefits – One of the most important benefits of this conversation is that it will get everyone on the same page in terms of your shared and unique experiences with the organization/group and will serve as a foundation for envisioning and planning for the future of your work together.

- Instructions – Please go over to the timeline and sign-in using the BLACK markers only. Then have a seat in one of the chairs in the semi-circle.
  - o Write your name on the timeline when you first became a part of this community (may be at birth).
  - o Then draw or write a few words to represent one pivotal event you remember in the history of this community, since that time.

Choose another point, after those first two and preferably within the last 5 – 10 years that you would consider another pivotal point. Draw or write a few words there.
   [Wait for all participants to sign-in before continuing.]

Facilitated Discussion

Starting with the person who has been in the community the longest and continuing across time, use prompting questions as needed to keep the conversation flowing and to draw out what is useful to understanding the history of the group/organization and the people involved:

Examples: What was the community like at that time? What was the larger world like at that time? What were young people like? What was the role of the elders during that time? What do you think created this [event/change/atmosphere,etc.]?
   [While this discussion is going on, one facilitator should be making notes on flipchart identifying "Aha" moments – interesting points that clarify important ideas, incidents, etc.]

Debrief the Discussion (Depending on how much time the discussion took and the proximity of the timeline to the other seating arrangement, it may be conducive to take a break before continuing or move to another seating area.)
Now we need to talk about what all this means.

- Let's look at "ah-has" we've identified so far (review).

- Any insights or "ah-has" other than what we captured on the flipchart?

- How would you complete the following sentence:
  - o This community has been a place where...
  - o This community/world has been a place where....
  - o The people involved with this room have....

- Given our current understanding of the past, let's think in terms of the future and ask:
  - o What "Take Forwards" or "Greatest Hopes" for the future would you like to list?
  - o What "Leave Behinds" or "Worst Fears" for the future would you like to list?

Wrap-Up/Transition: Great work, everyone! Now that we have a clearer, shared understanding of the history of this community, it's time to... (If enough time has passed since the last one, this would be a good time to take a break before continuing with the next part of the meeting.)

Gawa Kazi (Shared Work) Skills Assessment Sample

Our group and our community is blessed with an assortment of skills, talents, abilities and knowledge that we can build upon for the good of the entire community. The concept of GawaKazi (Shared Work), provides an opportunity for us to assess the skills available within our group, as well as those things that are need by other.

With such an assessment completed, we can determine the best ways to swap and share those skills with each other. Some groups/communities utilize some type of "community money" or sharing coupons, whereby individuals who receive services can "pay" those delivering the services. Subsequently, those who receive the coupons may exchange them for goods and/or services that they may need.

For example, you bring me a small basket full of apples. I give you a coupon for designing/tying a resume. You don't need a resume but you do need someone to help you weed your garden. A neighbor, who is seeking work, volunteers to assist with the garden. As "payment," (if she agrees), is the coupon for help with a resume. She may then, in turn, cash in the coupon with me, in order to get the resume completed.

Often we don't realize how many skills we actually have among us, never mind the types of services they can give and receive from other people that would help improve the lives of others. Frequently we take what we can do for granted and don't realize that something we do every day—driving, cooking, sewing, taking care of children and housecleaning, for example—could make a big difference in someone else's life.

This survey also helps communities get a sense of what kinds of services are too expensive or hard to find within the community.

Please circle "give" for the things you can do and "receive" for the things you'd like to get from other people. If you'd like to both give *and* receive something, don't hesitate to circle both.

Feel free to add to the list of you have gifts or needs that are not listed!

Health

Caring for the sick, elderly or disabled	Give	Receive
What did you do for them?		
Feeding and preparing special foods	Give	Receive
Bathing, grooming & dressing	Give	Receive
Companionship	Give	Receive
Fitness & Exercise: Yoga, Aerobics, Weight lifting	Give	Receive
Diet & Nutrition	Give	Receive

Massage & Complementary Therapies	Give	Receive
Mental Health Counseling	Give	Receive
Medical Services: Doctors, Chiropractors, Dentists	Give	Receive

Office & Professional

Typing, word processing, computer data entry	Give	Receive
Answering phones and taking messages	Give	Receive
Operating a switchboard	Give	Receive
Filing & keeping track of supplies	Give	Receive
Shorthand or speedwriting	Give	Receive
Writing business letters	Give	Receive
Bookkeeping	Give	Receive
Odd Jobs & running errands	Give	Receive
Operating a cash register	Give	Receive
Writing reports	Give	Receive
Managing other people	Give	Receive
Interviewing people	Give	Receive
Legal	Give	Receive
Product sales	Give	Receive
Telephone sales	Give	Receive
Door-to-door sales	Give	Receive
Security Guard or crowd control	Give	Receive

Home Maintenance & Repair

Housecleaning: mopping, washing windows, vacuuming, dusting	Give	Receive
Garden & Lawn Care: Weeding, mowing, planting, pruning	Give	Receive
Plumbing:		

Fixing leaky faucets, unclogging drains	Give	Receive
Installing appliances, faucets, and fixtures	Give	Receive

Walls & Floors:

Painting & wallpapering	Give	Receive
Knocking out walls	Give	Receive
Floor sanding or stripping	Give	Receive
Build room additions & install windows	Give	Receive
Install insulation	Give	Receive
Drywall & taping	Give	Receive
Install carpets	Give	Receive
Install wood floors	Give	Receive
Plastering	Give	Receive
Tile work	Give	Receive
Carpentry skills	Give	Receive
Cabinetmaking	Give	Receive
Roof repairs	Give	Receive
Electrical Repairs	Give	Receive
Appliance Repairs: Dishwashers, washers, dryers, refrigerators	Give	Receive
Bricklaying & Masonry	Give	Receive
Soldering & Welding	Give	Receive
Furniture Repair	Give	Receive
Installing/repairing heating & cooling system	Give	Receive
Repairing radios, TVs, VCRs, etc.	Give	Receive
Installing/repairing alarms or security systems	Give	Receive
Car maintenance	Give	Receive
Car repairs	Give	Receive

Food

Baking

Less than 10 people	Give	Receive
More than 10 people	Give	Receive

Preparing meals

Less than 10 people	Give	Receive
More than 10 people	Give	Receive

Clearing/Setting tables

Less than 10 people	Give	Receive
More than 10 people	Give	Receive

Washing Dishes

Less than 10 people	Give	Receive
More than 10 people	Give	Receive
Bartending	Give	Receive
Catering	Give	Receive

Family Care

Caring for babies under a year	Give	Receive
Caring for kids 1 to 6	Give	Receive
Caring for kids 7 to 13	Give	Receive
Working with teens	Give	Receive
Caring for elderly parents	Give	Receive
Taking groups of people on field trips	Give	Receive
Pet care	Give	Receive

Transportation

Driving a car or van	Give	Receive
Driving a school bus	Give	Receive
Driving a taxi	Give	Receive
Delivery work	Give	Receive

Running errands	Give	Receive

Other

Sewing	Give	Receive
Upholstering	Give	Receive
Dressmaking and/or tailoring	Give	Receive
Knitting and/or crocheting	Give	Receive
House and furniture moving (and packing)	Give	Receive
Assisting in the classroom	Give	Receive
Hair dressing and/or cutting	Give	Receive
Doing phone surveys	Give	Receive

Music

Singing	Give	Receive
Do you play an instrument? (Which one)	Give	Receive

Community

Have you ever organized or participated in any of the following community activities? Please check the ones that apply and write yes if you would like to participate in any of them again in the future.

Boy Scouts/Girl Scouts

Church or community organization fundraisers

Bingo
Rummage or yard sales
Church suppers
Parent-Teacher Organizations

Sports Teams – coaching or playing

Camping trips with kids

Field trips

Political campaigns

Community gardens

Neighborhood clean-ups

Community groups

Other groups or community work

Priority Skills

After going through the above list of different skills, please try answering the following questions.

What three things do you think you do best?

Are there any skills you'd like to teach?

Are there any skills you'd like to learn?

Council of Elders Meeting
[Date]
[Location]

AGENDA

1. **Opening Rituals – Libations, etc.**

2. **Review of Agreements/Commitments from Last Meeting**

Agreements from Past Meetings		
Who	**What**	**By When**

3. **Today's Meeting Agenda Items (Include regular discussion items)**

   Item 1. Old/Unresolved Business from last meeting not included above (Itemize)
   Item 2. Commission Reports (if any)
   Item 3. New Business (Itemize)
   Item 4. Treasurer's Report
   Item 5. Final Review of Agreements from current meeting

4. **Today's Agreements**

Past Agreements		
Who	**What**	**By When**

Next Meeting
[Date, Time, Location]

1. Review of Past Agreements
2. Regular and New Meeting Agenda Items

www.ingramcontent.com/pod-product-compliance
Lightning Source LLC
Chambersburg PA
CBHW081359280526
45788CB00009B/2929